OECD Studies on Water

Implementing the OECD Principles on Water Governance

INDICATOR FRAMEWORK AND EVOLVING PRACTICES

OECD

BETTER POLICIES FOR BETTER LIVES

This document, as well as any data and any map included herein, are without prejudice to the status of or sovereignty over any territory, to the delimitation of international frontiers and boundaries and to the name of any territory, city or area.

Please cite this publication as:
OECD (2018), *Implementing the OECD Principles on Water Governance: Indicator Framework and Evolving Practices*, OECD Studies on Water, OECD Publishing, Paris.
http://dx.doi.org/10.1787/9789264292659-en

ISBN 978-92-64-29266-6 (print)
ISBN 978-92-64-29265-9 (PDF)

Series: OECD Studies on Water
ISSN 2224-5073 (print)
ISSN 2224-5081 (online)

The statistical data for Israel are supplied by and under the responsibility of the relevant Israeli authorities. The use of such data by the OECD is without prejudice to the status of the Golan Heights, East Jerusalem and Israeli settlements in the West Bank under the terms of international law.

Photo credits: Cover © Taro Yamada/Corbis; © AridOcean/Shutterstock.com

Corrigenda to OECD publications may be found on line at: *www.oecd.org/about/publishing/corrigenda.htm.*

Preface

We, representatives of river basin organisations, science, policy think tanks, regional water authorities, representatives of public and private water service providers, and non-governmental organisations, are delighted to introduce the results of our collective engagement over the last three years to support the implementation of the *OECD Principles on Water Governance*.

Actually, our journey started in 2012 at the 6th World Water Forum in France. At the time, we actively contributed to the OECD-led Core Group on "Good Governance" for the Forum. And it is as a follow-up to this collective approach that we co-founded the multi-stakeholder OECD Water Governance Initiative (WGI) in March 2013 to continue to join forces for better water policies for better lives.

After three years of collaborative development of the *OECD Principles on Water Governance* (2013-15), we enlarged the group of champion countries and institutions and catalysed further support at the 7th World Water Forum (Korea, April 2015), with over 60 organisations from the public, private and non-profit sectors signing the "Daegu Multi-stakeholder Declaration" and committing to use the OECD Principles in their activities and practices.

Over 2015-18, we have maintained this active co-operation and achieved another important milestone with the indicator framework and evolving stories contained in this report. While we are aware that this is work in progress, we are particularly proud of the inclusive and bottom-up approach inherent to the development of these tools and herein call for a massive and widespread use of the indicator framework as a voluntary self-assessment tool and the water governance practices to facilitate the sharing of experiences and bench-learning.

We look forward to our continued co-operation and stand ready to build greater capacities on how to apply the Principles as a vehicle for policy dialogues on the road to the 9th World Water Forum in Senegal in 2021, and as a contribution towards achieving the 2030 Agenda for Sustainable Development and other international commitments.

Great progress has been made so far, but a lot more remains to be done to cope with current and future water crises, which ultimately are often governance crises.

The OECD Water Governance Initiative Steering Committee

Peter Glas, Chair

Alejandro Jimenez, Stockholm International Water Institute

Donal O'Leary, Transparency International

Eric Tardieu, International Office for Water

Jean Francois Donzier International Network of Basin Organisations

Gari Villa-Landa Sokolova, Spanish Association of Water Supply and Sanitation

Joannie Leclerc, SUEZ

Pierre-Alain Roche, Scientific and Technical Association for Water and the Environment, France

Teun Bastemeijer, Water Integrity Network

Daniel Valensuela, International Network of Basin Organisations

Foreword

As a result of three years of work to support the implementation of the *OECD Principles on Water Governance* adopted by the OECD Regional Development Committee in 2015, this report proposes two supporting tools for interested cities, regions and countries to improve their water policies. First, the Water Governance Indicator Framework is intended as a voluntary and self-assessment tool to engage in multi-stakeholder dialogues on the performance of water governance systems. Second, a set of 54 evolving practices seek to provide a source of inspiration and stimulation for bench-learning. These supporting tools were produced through a bottom-up and multi stakeholder process within the OECD Water Governance Initiative, reflecting collective views, opinions and experiences.

This report seeks to support governments and stakeholders in addressing challenges and pressures from megatrends on water demand and supply through more effective institutions. Climate change, economic growth, urbanisation and growing populations affect water availability and quality now and will do so even more in the future. Both OECD and non-OECD countries are increasingly exposed to economic losses due to flood risk, droughts and degrading water quality of surface- and ground-water resources. Significant investments are needed to renew or upgrade infrastructure for water supply and sanitation, with increasing additional pressures from manufacturing, energy and irrigation.

This report recalls the need for effective, efficient and inclusive governance, and for better understanding who does what, at which level, how and why with respect to water-related policies. Indeed, technical solutions to water-related challenges often exist and are well-known; what is challenging to put them into practice is the policy environment. The implementation of water laws, regulations and policies, as well as policy alignment across sectors, remain a challenge in both OECD and non-OECD countries from local to national levels. Governance systems with insufficient integrity and transparency may also hinder safe and clean access to water services and water security for all.

Governments and stakeholders are invited to make the most of the proposed indicator framework for collectively identifying policies and strategies that can better manage water challenges. Although much still remains to be done to propose a comprehensive framework for assessing water governance, the tools herein provided are a first concrete achievement that can significantly contribute to the development of better water policies for better lives.

Acknowledgements

This report is the outcome of three years of bottom-up and multi-stakeholder work in close co-operation with the OECD Water Governance Initiative (WGI) to support the implementation of the *OECD Principles on Water Governance* adopted by the OECD Regional Development Policy Committee on 11 May 2015 and backed by ministers at the OECD Ministerial Council Meeting of 3-4 June 2015. This project was developed by the OECD Centre for Entrepreneurship, SMEs, Regions and Cities (CFE) led by Lamia Kamal-Chaoui, Director, and as part of the 2017-18 programme of work of the Regional Development Policy Committee.

The underlying policy dialogues and activities were managed by Aziza Akhmouch, Acting Head of the Cities, Urban Policies and Sustainable Development Division in CFE. The report was co-ordinated and drafted by a core team led by Håkan Tropp, Head of the Water Governance Programme (Chapter 1) with Oriana Romano, Policy Analyst (Chapter 2) and Antonio Cañamás Catalá, Junior Policy Analyst (Chapter 3). The report also includes inputs from Delphine Clavreul (analysis of evolving practices) and Natalia Altman (analysis of pilot test results) from the OECD Secretariat.

The Secretariat is grateful to the members of the WGI Steering Committee, chaired by Peter Glas, for their excellent support and commitment throughout the process, in particular the co-leaders of the Working Group on Indicators: Pierre-Alain Roche (Scientific and Technical Association for Water and the Environment, France), Jean-Francois Donzier and Daniel Valensuela (International Network of Basin Organisations), Eric Tardieu (International Office for Water) and Donal O'Leary (Transparency International); as well as the co-leaders of the Working Group on Best Practices: Joannie Leclerc (SUEZ), Teun Bastemeijer (Water Integrity Network) and Jenny Grönwall (Stockholm International Water Institute).

The Secretariat is also grateful for the tireless efforts of lead institutions that pilot tested the draft indicator framework: Guillermo Avanzini Pinto and Soraya Gina Salcedo Janampa (National Water Authority, Peru); Samira El Haouat (Sebou River Basin, Morocco); Teodoro Estrela Monreal, Tatiana Ortega Gómez, Maria Serneguet Belda and Laura Tanco Ballesteros (Jucar River Basin, Spain); Manfred Eisenhut (Association for Water and Gas, Austria) and Marcus Heiss (Association of Public Services and Enterprises Austria); Barry Greig, Craig McGill and Jon Rathjen (Scotland, United Kingdom); Gerald Jan Ellen, Henriette Otter and Nishchal Sardjoe (Deltares, Netherlands) and Anoeska Buijze, Herman Kasper Gilissen (Utrecht University); Gari Villa-Landa Sokolova (Spanish Association of Water Supply and Sanitation, Segura River Basin); Nor Zamri Bin Sondor (Selangor Water Management Authority, Malaysia) with the support of Tadashige Kawasaki (Network of Asian River Basin Organizations and Japan Water Agency); Maria Ximena Barrera Rey, Pablo Montes Iannini and Dora Milena Zapata Grajales (World Wildlife Fund, Rio Nare River Basin, Colombia); François Brikké (Global Water Partnership) and Eugène Shamba Nzitatira (Democratic Republic of Congo Water Partnership); Vladimir Arana (International Secretariat for

Water, Rimac River Basin, Peru); and Hercules Vieira (National Agency for Water And Sanitation, Cabo Verde) with the support of Francisco Nunes Correia and Larissa Varela (Instituto Superior Técnico, Lisbon). The Secretariat also thanks Cristina Novo, Carine Morin-Batut and Daniel Valensuela for translating the pilot-tested indicator framework and results into Spanish and French.

Special thanks are herein conveyed to the 54 promoters of evolving water governance practices (Table 3.2): Flanders Knowledge Center Water (Vlakwa, Belgium); Ministry of Environmental Protection (Israel); Federal Ministry of Agriculture, Forestry, Environment and Water Management (Austria); Vienna Water – City of Vienna (Austria); SUEZ; Global Water Partnership; Segura River Basin Authority (Segura River Basin Authority, Spain); Fundación Instituto Tecnológico de Galicia (Spain); Madjulla Inc. (Australia); Regional Water Authority De Dommel (Netherlands); Palestinian Water Authority; Alliance for Global Water Adaptation; ebswien hauptkläranlage Ges.m.b.H. (Austria); Association for Gas and Water (Austria); AQUAE (Spain); Universitat Politècnica de Catalunya (Spain); Water and Waste Services Regulation Authority (Portugal); Utrecht University, Centre for Water, Oceans and Sustainability Law (Netherlands); Environmental Protection Agency (Ireland); Dutch Water Authorities; ACCIONA Agua (Spain); Regional Council Tübingen (Germany); Initiative Développement (France); United Nations Development Programme; Jasa Tirta I Public Coorporation (Indonesia); Japan Water Agency; Syndicat des eaux et de l'assainissement Alsace-Moselle (France); The Nature Conservancy; World Wildlife Fund México; Conseil régional de Bretagne (France); Gesellschaft für Internationale Zusammenarbeit (Germany); International Commission for the Protection of the Rhine; K-water Institute (Korea); Programme Solidarité-Eau; Environmental Advocacy Center of Panama; Institute for Economic and Environmental Policy (Czech Republic); Regulatory Agency for Water, Energy and Basic Sanitation (Brazil); Turkish Ministry of Forestry and Water Affairs and Turkish Water Institute; Rare (Colombia); Australian National University; and the International Commission for the Protection of the Danube River.

The authors are grateful to Kevin Collins (The Open University), Sarah Hendry (University of Dundee) and Sophie Richard (AgroParisTech) for their contribution to the overarching analysis of evolving practices on water governance, and Maelis Monnier (SUEZ) for her comments on early drafts of the overarching analysis; as well as to the hosts of peer-to-peer webinars where they were discussed, namely Dirk Halet (Flanders Knowledge Center Water, Belgium), Danny Greenwald (Israel Water Authority), Joannie Leclerc (SUEZ), and Ernst Überreiter (Federal Ministry of Agriculture, Forestry, Environment and Water Management, Austria) and Marcus Heiss (Association of Public Services and Enterprises, Austria).

The Secretariat is grateful to the respondents to the survey on the OECD Principles (Annex 1.A1) and the survey on best practices (Annex 3.A1), to the 11 institutions (the Australian National University, the European Centre of Employers and Enterprises providing Public Services and Services of general interest, International Association for Water Law, KWR Watercycle Research Institute, Madrid Institute of Advanced Studies, Shepherd and Wedderburn, the Spanish Association of Water Supply and Sanitation, the Stockholm International Water Institute, Utrecht University, Water Integrity Network, and the World Health Organization) who submitted proposals for water governance indicators and to the more than 170 members of the Coalition for Good Water Governance who committed to share their achievements and good practices on water governance; disseminate the *OECD Principles on Water Governance* to their constituencies, members and networks; and report back on how they use the Principles to guide their activities and practices.

Earlier versions of the report were discussed in a series of webinars (25 April 2016, 15 November 2016, 25 November 2016, 15 June 2017) and at the 9th (3-4 July 2017, Paris) and 10th (20-21 November, Vienna, hosted by the Austrian Association of Cities and Towns) meetings of the OECD Water Governance Initiative. For their written comments and suggestions, special thanks are given to: Céline Kauffmann and Karen Maguire from OECD Secretariat; the Spanish Association of Water Supply and Sanitation; Dutch Water Authorities; the Dutch Ministry of Infrastructure and Water Management; the Portuguese Water and Waste Services Regulation Authority; the Federal Ministry of Agriculture, Forestry, Environment and Water Management, Austria; Butterfly Effect; International Water Association; the Network of Asian River Basin Organizations; Peter Gammeltoft (expert); Stockholm International Water Institute; SUEZ; Transparency International; the Association of Public Services and Enterprises, Austria; United Nations Educational, Scientific and Cultural Organization; the University of Arizona; and the Water Integrity Network. Throughout the year, the substantive components of this manuscript were shared for comments with delegates of the OECD Regional Development Policy Committee, which approved the final report through written procedure on 5 March 2018. The report benefited from valuable editorial guidance from Janine Treves. It was edited by Caitlin Connelly and formatted by Jennifer Allain. Cicely Dupont-Nivore prepared the manuscript for publication.

Table of contents

Tables

Figures

Boxes

Acronyms and abbreviations

AEAS	Spanish Association of Water Supply and Sanitation (Spain) *Asociación Española de Abastecimientos de Agua y Saneamiento*
ERSAR	Portuguese Water and Waste Services Regulation Authority *Entidade Reguladora dos Serviços de Águas e Resíduos*
EU	European Union
FAO	Food and Agriculture Organization
GIS	Geographic information system
GIZ	German Agency for International Co-operation *Gesellschaft für Internationale Zusammenarbeit*
GWP	Global Water Partnership
INBO/OIEau	International Network of Basin Organisations/*Office International de l'Eau*
IWA	International Water Association
IWRM	Integrated water resources management
NARBO	Network of Asian River Basin Organizations
NCWR	Non-conventional water resources
NGO	Non-governmental organisation
NWIS	National Water Information System (Turkey)
OECD	Organisation for Economic Co-operation and Development
ONEMA	National Agency for Water and Aquatic Environments (France) *Office National Eau Milieux Aquatiques*
ÖVGW	Austrian Association for Water & Gas *Österreichische Vereinigung für das Gas- und Wasserfach*
PES	Payments for ecosystem services
pS-Eau	Water Solidarity Programme
SDEA Alsace Moselle	*Syndicat des eaux et de l'assainissement Alsace-Moselle* (France)
SDG	Sustainable Development Goal
SIWI	Stockholm International Water Institute
UN-Habitat	United Nations Human Settlements Programme
UN-Water	United Nations Water
UNDP	United Nations Development Programme

UNESCO	United Nations Educational, Scientific and Cultural Organization
WASH	Water, sanitation and hygiene
WFD	Water Framework Directive
WGI	Water Governance Initiative
WIN	Water Integrity Network
WWF	World Wildlife Fund

Executive summary

Good water management is critical to sustainable development and to people's well-being because of its pivotal role for economic growth, social inclusion and environmental sustainability. An increasing number of countries, OECD members and non-members alike, are facing mounting challenges to manage effectively too little, too much and too polluted waters, and to sustain universal coverage of drinking water and sanitation services due to massive investment backlogs in infrastructure and difficulties to maintain and operate existing assets.

Several mega-trends are affecting the way cities, regions and countries are able to manage their water resources and services now and in the future, in particular the impact of climate change on water supply and demand, and pressures arising from demographic trends such as population growth, migration and urbanisation. Good water governance can greatly contribute to the design and implementation of policy and practice, in a shared responsibility across levels of government, civil society, business and the broader range of stakeholders who have an important role to play alongside policy makers. This requires going beyond the "what to do?" to also consider "who does what?", "why?", "at which level of government?" and "how?". If water challenges are not addressed properly within integrated social, environmental, economic and sectoral policies, the achievement of, for example, the Sustainable Development Goals (SDGs), the Paris Agreement or the Sendai Framework, will be in jeopardy.

In 2015, the *OECD Principles on Water Governance* emphasised that policy responses to water challenges will only be viable if they are coherent and integrated; if stakeholders are properly engaged; if well-designed regulatory frameworks are in place; if there is adequate and accessible information; and if there is sufficient capacity, integrity and transparency. While framing the key conditions for effective, efficient and inclusive water policies, the Principles provide a tool for dialogue to understand whether water governance systems are performing optimally and where change, reforms or actions are needed.

Three years after the adoption of the Principles, this report takes stock on their use and provides an indicator framework and a set of evolving practices, building on lessons learnt from their implementation and application in different countries and contexts. These tools are the result of an extensive bottom-up and multi-stakeholder process within the OECD Water Governance Initiative. They are conceived as voluntary methodologies that can be used and contextualised by interested cities, regions, basins and countries to improve their water sector policies and strategies.

A survey conducted across the 170 stakeholders having endorsed the Principles, gathered within the Global Coalition for Good Water Governance, shows that 80% of the respondents have been using the Principles to facilitate multi-stakeholder dialogue, assess water governance performance, guide reform processes and practices, build capacities, and/or develop research (Chapter 1). Respondents also emphasised the high potential to further support the uptake and implementation of the Principles by governments and other stakeholders in support of, for example, national sector goals linked to the Sustainable

Development Goals, and to make use of and develop tools and build more capacity on how to apply the Principles as a vehicle for policy dialogue and practical assessment, among others.

The Water Governance Indicator Framework (Chapter 2) is conceived as a voluntary self-assessment tool to assess the state of play of water governance policy frameworks (what), institutions (who) and instruments (how), and their needed improvements over time. It is intended to be applicable across governance scales (local, basin, national, etc.) and water functions (water resources management, water services provisioning and water disaster risk reduction). It is grounded on a sound bottom-up and multi-stakeholder approach rather than a reporting, monitoring or benchmarking perspective, since governance responses to common water challenges are highly contextual and place-based. Its primary objective is to stimulate a transparent, neutral, open, inclusive and forward-looking dialogue across stakeholders on what works, what does not, what should be improved and who can do what. To support the indicator framework's end-users, this report provides guidance to carry out the self-assessment in ten steps, before, during and after the assessment. The indicator framework is composed of a traffic light system based on 36 input and process indicators and a checklist with questions on a number of more specific governance conditions. It concludes with an action plan to prepare and prioritise actions over the short, medium and long run.

The evolving water governance practices (Chapter 3) are meant to help policy makers, practitioners and other stakeholders learn from each other and identify pitfalls to avoid when designing and implementing water policies. As such, they are a vehicle for peer-to-peer dialogue and learning. Collected amongst members of the Water Governance Initiative and the Global Coalition for Good Water Governance, the 54 practices were analysed at face value to showcase how water governance works in practice across geographical context, scales (international, national, regional, basin, local), time frames (from less than a year to more than ten years), actors involved and water functions. Three critical elements are common to the success of all these practices: stakeholder engagement, financing and political will. The practices show that improved water governance generates positive welfare effects on social and environmental well-being and sustained economic growth.

In conclusion, the tools proposed in this report are means, amongst a broader menu of options, to support interested countries in self-assessing and improving the performance of their water governance system and to stimulate collective learning and peer support among governments and stakeholders around the world. Since governance is a means to an end, and implies dynamic processes and strategies to adapt to changing circumstances, needs and demands, this implementation framework is primarily conceived as a first contribution to support further implementation of the *OECD Principles on Water Governance*, and should be considered work in progress towards future refinements. In fact, while indicators can raise awareness and address information asymmetries as a step towards better water governance, there is no unique way to measure the complexity that the concept of water governance entails, or to capture the variety of water governance dimensions, and the diversity of political, historical, legal, administrative, geographic and economic circumstances. The process of collective assessment can in and of itself be a way to progress, as open and inclusive assessments can reveal potential governance gaps and disagreements among stakeholders and find ways on how to address them.

Chapter 1.

OECD Principles on Water Governance: Taking stock

This chapter describes the rationale, process and content of the OECD Principles on Water Governance. *The Principles provide a framework to understand whether water governance systems are performing optimally and to help adjust them where necessary. A number of examples show that the Principles have been applied across difference scales, stakeholders and sectors, either as a tool to understand how water governance systems are performing at local, basin or national level, or as a reading template to guide decisions for water stakeholders and institutions on specific water functions. The chapter concludes with the results of a survey carried out across members of the OECD Water Governance Initiative and the broader Global Coalition for Good Water Governance on the use and dissemination of the Principles.*

Water: A driver for sustainable development

Water is a pivotal driver to economic growth, and improved social and environmental well-being. An increasing number of countries are facing mounting challenges of too little, too much or too polluted waters. These bring with them serious implications to meeting other societal objectives, such as safe drinking water supply, wastewater management, food and energy security, improved health, sustainable ecosystems, poverty eradication, and sustained economic growth. Water scarcity, water disasters and extreme weather events, such as floods and droughts, and failures of climate change mitigation and adaptation, rank as top global risks as assessed in the World Economic Forum's *Global Risk Report* (World Economic Forum, 2018). They also threaten to have the most severe potential impacts on social and economic well-being.

The effects of climate change, economic growth, urbanisation and growing populations, among others, continue to drive water availability and quality now and in the future. Accessible and high-quality freshwater is a limited and highly variable resource in space and time. OECD projections show that 40% of the world's population currently lives in water-stressed river basins, and that water demand will rise by 55% by 2050 (OECD, 2012). Over-abstraction and contamination of aquifers worldwide is posing significant challenges to food security, the health of ecosystems and safe drinking water supply. In 2050, 240 million people are expected to remain without access to clean water, and 1.4 billion without access to basic sanitation, despite global efforts to tackle this shortage. Significant investment is required to renew and upgrade infrastructure, estimated at USD 6.7 trillion by 2050 for water supply and sanitation, and including a wider range of water-related infrastructure that could triple that cost by 2030 (OECD, 2015). For example, flood risks are anticipated to rise rapidly in both OECD countries and non-OECD economies with great potential for the loss of human life and property. India faces the highest economic risks of flooding, followed by the People's Republic of China and Viet Nam respectively. Flooding is also expected to increase rapidly in Europe and North America. The United States is projected to have the greatest economic exposure to flood risk in the world, with expected annual property damage from flooding estimated at USD 54 billion (Sadoff et al., 2015).

The achievement of internationally agreed Sustainable Development Goals (SDGs) and targets will require that water challenges be addressed, not only as part of the water-dedicated SDG 6 "Water and Sanitation for All", but also as part of other SDGs related to sustainable production and consumption patterns, sustainable cities, improved health, and energy and food security, etc. Similarly, it will be critical to address water challenges as part of achieving the New Urban Agenda, the Paris Climate Agreement and the Sendai Framework for Disaster Risk Reduction 2015-2030, which explicitly calls for "strengthening disaster risk governance to manage disaster risk". Meeting the nationally determined contributions on water adaptation under the Paris Climate Agreement and the Sendai Framework requires improved national policy alignment across sectors and governance scales. A particular challenge in these internationally agreed development frameworks is that governance in relation to water is either included in a very piecemeal fashion or not included at all. Out of the eight SDG 6 targets and indicators, two of them are defined as "means of implementation" and relate to international co-operation and capacity building (Target 6.a) and participation of local communities in improving water and sanitation management (Target 6.b). Target 6.5 aims to implement integrated water resources management at all levels. At best, the New Urban Agenda, the Paris Climate

Agreement and the Sendai Framework address water governance indirectly; they all refer to water and to governance, but they do not combine them.

While global water challenges persist, current levels of service delivery and water security in OECD and non-OECD economies cannot be taken for granted. Actions are needed at multiple levels of government and across sectors. The technical solutions to water-related challenges often exist and are well-known. The policy environment, however, can be a barrier to putting them into practice, which requires effectiveness, efficiency and inclusiveness in terms governance of who does what, at which level, how and why. Existing governance systems are often not equipped to cope with increasing water demands and climate variability, degrading ecosystems, and water-related natural disasters. The implementation of water laws, regulations and policies, as well as policy alignment across sectors, remain a challenge in both OECD countries and non-OECD economies, from local to national levels.

Why good water governance matters

Water crises are oftentimes rooted in governance crises. The water sector holds intrinsic characteristics that make it highly sensitive to and dependent on multi-level governance, and some of the sector's features are susceptible to governance failures:

- Water connects across sectors, places and people, as well as geographic and temporal scales. In most cases, hydrological boundaries and administrative perimeters do not coincide.
- Freshwater management (surface and groundwater) is both a global and local concern, and involves a plethora of public, private and non-profit stakeholders in the decision-making, policy and project cycles.
- Water is a highly capital-intensive and monopolistic sector, with important market failures where co-ordination is essential.
- Water policy is inherently complex and strongly linked to domains that are critical for development, including health, environment, agriculture, energy, spatial planning, regional development and poverty alleviation.
- To varying degrees, countries have allocated increasingly complex and resource-intensive responsibilities to subnational governments, resulting in interdependencies across levels of government that require co-ordination to mitigate fragmentation.

Coping with future water challenges raises not only the question of "what to do?", but also "who does what?", "why?", "at which level of government?" and "how?". Policy responses will only be viable if they are coherent; if stakeholders are properly engaged; if well-designed regulatory frameworks are in place; if there is adequate and accessible information; and if there is sufficient capacity, integrity and transparency. To be fit for the future, institutions need to adapt to changing circumstances, and political will and policy continuity are key in the transition towards more inclusive and sustainable practices. However, the water sector usually is exposed to several governance "gaps" that can reinforce each other if not properly addressed (Figure 1.1; OECD, 2011). These include:

- Institutional and territorial fragmentation of water policy across multiple actors and lack of effective policy coherence across sectors (policy gap).

- Mismatch across administrative and hydrological boundaries to manage water resources and supply water services at the relevant scale (administrative gap).
- Questionable resource allocation and patchy financial management (funding gap).
- Gaps in knowledge, human capital, technology and other capabilities to design and implement sustainable, efficient and effective water policies (capacity gap).
- Ineffective stakeholder engagement for inclusive and transparent decision making; lack of or not regular use of monitoring, evaluation and enforcement mechanisms (accountability gap).
- Divergent objectives that inhibit synergies and complementarities at the right scale (objective gap).
- Insufficient or incomplete water information systems in support of decision makers (information gap).

Figure 1.1. **OECD Multi-Level Governance Framework: "Mind the gaps, bridge the gaps"**

Source: OECD (2011), *Water Governance in OECD Countries: A Multi-level Approach*, http://dx.doi.org/10.1787/9789264119284-en.

Any well-functioning water governance system should be able to manage water quantity and quality to ensure, for example, public health and food and energy security and sustainable ecosystems. It should also provide rationales for whom and what purposes water is provided. There is no one-size-fits-all governance response to the water challenge worldwide, but a huge diversity of situations within and across countries that need to be taken into account.

Governance is a means to an end, and the type of governance should match the level of risk or the magnitude of the problem to fit policies to places. Governance needs to be adaptive, context-dependent and place-based in order to take into account historical and territorial specificities and challenges. The OECD defines water governance as the "range of political, institutional and administrative rules, practices and processes (formal and informal) through which decisions are taken and implemented, stakeholders can articulate their interests and have their concerns considered, and decision makers are held accountable for water management" (OECD, 2015). In other words, governance addresses the role of institutions and relationships between organisations and social groups involved in water decision making, both horizontally across sectors and between urban and rural areas, and vertically from local to international levels. As such, governance is much broader than government as it also seeks to include the private sector, civil society and a wide range of stakeholders with a stake in water use and management.

The *OECD Principles on Water Governance*

In May 2015, the *OECD Principles on Water Governance* were adopted by the OECD Regional Development Policy Committee[1] and backed by ministers at the OECD Council Meeting at Ministerial Level in June 2015. Subsequently, a Global Coalition for Good Water Governance[2] was created to convene all OECD member countries and non-OECD economies, as well as stakeholder groups that endorsed the Principles and intended to use them to guide their activities and practices. The Global Coalition for Good Water Governance aims to trigger collective action and to guide public action from policy makers, civil society, business and society at large through the identification, collection and upscaling of water governance solutions. A year and a half after their adoption, the *OECD Principles on Water Governance* were included in Section 6 of the *OECD Council Recommendation on Water* adopted in December 2016 as a new OECD legal instrument to guide better water policies and reforms.

Rationale

Coping with current and future water challenges requires robust public policies targeting measurable objectives along pre-determined time schedules and at the appropriate scale, a clear assignment of duties across responsible authorities, and regular monitoring and evaluation. Water governance can greatly contribute to the design and implementation of such policies in a shared responsibility across levels of government, civil society, business and the broader range of stakeholders who have an important role to play alongside policy makers to reap the economic, social and environmental benefits of good water governance.

The Principles are rooted in broader good governance principles: legitimacy, transparency, accountability, human rights, rule of law and inclusiveness. As such, they consider water governance as a means to an end rather than an end in itself. The range of political, institutional and administrative rules, practices and processes (formal and informal) through which decisions are taken and implemented allow stakeholders to articulate their interests and to have their concerns considered, while decision makers are held accountable for water management.

The Principles consider that water governance systems (more or less formal, complex and costly) should be designed according to the challenges they are required to address. This problem-solving approach means that "forms" of water governance should follow "functions" of water governance. Structuring, institutionalising and/or formalising institutions should not detract from the ultimate objective of delivering sufficient water of good quality, while maintaining or improving the ecological integrity of water bodies.

The Principles argue that governance is not "good" or "bad" for theoretical or conceptual reasons but rather a neutral concept and primarily a means to an end. In practice, governance is good if it can help to solve key water challenges, using a combination of bottom-up and top-down processes while fostering constructive state-society relations. It is bad if it generates undue transaction costs and does not respond to place-based needs (OECD, 2015).

Process

The *OECD Principles on Water Governance* were developed and discussed through a bottom-up and multi-stakeholder process within the OECD Water Governance Initiative (WGI) (Box 1.1), under the umbrella and guidance of the OECD Regional Development Policy Committee, and in close co-operation with the OECD Regulatory Policy Committee and its Network of Economic Regulators. In addition, a range of OECD committees and subsidiary bodies carried out extensive consultation, including the Environment Policy Committee and its Working Party on Biodiversity, Water and Ecosystems, the Public Governance Committee and its Working Party of Senior Public Integrity Officials, the Development Assistance Committee; the Committee on Investment, and the Committee on Agriculture.

The Principles are based on the following considerations:

- Meeting current and future water challenges requires robust public policies targeting measurable objectives along pre-determined time schedules at the appropriate scale, a clear assignment of duties across responsible authorities, and regular monitoring and evaluation.
- Effective, efficient and inclusive water governance contributes to the design and implementation of such policies, in a shared responsibility across levels of government, and in co-operation with the relevant stakeholders to meet current and future water challenges.
- There cannot be a single, uniform policy response to the water challenges worldwide given the diversity of situations within and across countries in terms of legal and institutional frameworks, cultural practices, as well as climatic, geographic and economic conditions at the origin of diverse water challenges and policy responses.
- Water governance is an important component of the overall framework of water policies. Broader principles of good governance apply to the water sector, and water governance outcomes can also be contingent on progress in other domains of the water policy framework.
- These Principles are relevant for all levels of government and could be disseminated widely within interested member and non-member countries.

Content

The *OECD Principles on Water Governance* (Figure 1.3) provide a framework to understand whether water governance systems are performing optimally and to help adjust them where necessary. They can catalyse efforts for making good practices more visible, learning from international experience, and setting reform processes into motion at all levels of government to facilitate change where and when needed. They can also help avoid traps and pitfalls, learning from international experience.

Box 1.1. The OECD Water Governance Initiative

The OECD Water Governance Initiative (WGI) was created on 27-28 March 2013. It gathers twice a year in a policy forum to share experience on water reforms, peer review analytical work on water governance, and produce bottom-up knowledge and guidance. It has several objectives (Figure 1.2):

- provide a multi-stakeholder technical platform to share knowledge, experience and best practices on water governance across levels of government
- advise governments in taking the needed steps for effective water reforms through peer-to-peer dialogue and stakeholder engagement across public, private and non-profit sectors
- provide a consultation mechanism to raise the profile of governance on the global water agenda (Sustainable Development Goals, World Water Forum, Habitat III, COP, etc.)
- support the implementation of the *OECD Principles on Water Governance* in interested member and non-member countries, basins and cities by scaling-up best practices and developing indicators
- foster continuity on governance discussions at a global level, in particular by supporting the Implementation Roadmap on Governance of the 7th World Water Forum (Korea, 2015) up to the 8th World Water Forum (Brazil, 2018).

Figure 1.2. **Water Governance Initiative objectives for the period 2016-18**

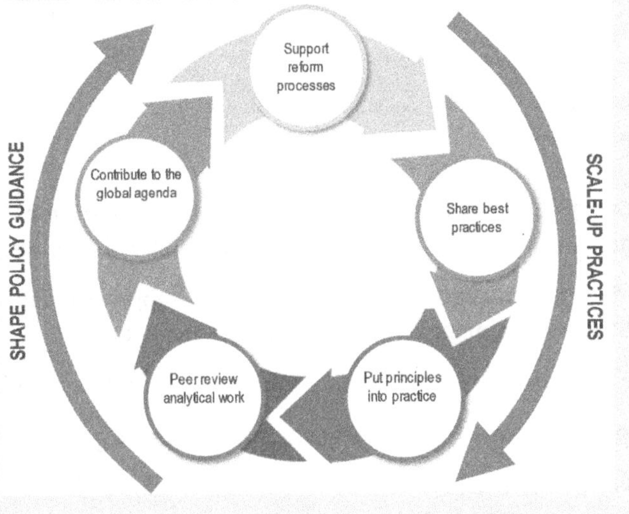

Its more than 130 members include national governments, basin and local authorities (and their networks), regulators (and their networks), donors and international financial institutions, non-governmental organisations, international organisations and institutions, service providers (both public and private, and their networks), as well as academics and independent experts. A Steering Committee supports the implementation of the strategic goals. It is composed of co-founding institutions, namely the International Network of Basin Organisations (INBO), Transparency International, the French Scientific and Technical Association for Water and Environment (*Association scientifique et technique pour l'eau et l'environnement*, ASTEE), SUEZ, Stockholm International Water Institute (SIWI) and the Water Integrity Network (WIN), and more recently the Spanish Association of Water Supply and Sanitation (*Asociación Española de Abastecimientos de Agua y Saneamiento*, AEAS). The Steering Committee is presided by a chair who is nominated every three years. Activities are implemented by working groups. During the triennium 2016-18, the two working groups contributed to the implementation strategy of the *OECD Principles on Water Governance*, focusing respectively on developing indicators and collecting and reviewing water governance stories.

Source: OECD (2016), "OECD Water Governance Initiative: Terms of reference 2016-18".

Figure 1.3. ***OECD Principles on Water Governance***

Source: OECD (2015), *OECD Principles on Water Governance*, www.oecd.org/governance/oecd-principles-on-water-governance.htm.

The Principles apply to the overarching water policy cycle and should be implemented in a systemic and inclusive manner. As such, they do not make distinctions across:

- water management functions (e.g. drinking water supply, sanitation, flood protection, water quality, water quantity, rainwater and storm-water)
- water uses (e.g. domestic, industry, agriculture, energy and environment)
- ownership of water management, resources and assets (e.g. public, private, mixed).

The Principles are clustered around three main dimensions (Box 2).

1. Effectiveness of water governance relates to the contribution of governance to defining clear sustainable water policy goals and targets at different levels of government, to implement those policy goals, and to meet expected objectives or targets.
2. Efficiency of water governance relates to the contribution of governance to maximising the benefits of sustainable water management and welfare at the least cost to society.
3. Trust and engagement in water governance relate to the contribution of governance to building public confidence and ensuring inclusiveness of stakeholders through democratic legitimacy and fairness for society at large.

Box 1.2. The *OECD Principles on Water Governance*

1. Clearly allocate and distinguish roles and responsibilities for water policy making, policy implementation, operational management and regulation, and foster co-ordination across these responsible authorities.
2. Manage water at the appropriate scale(s) within integrated basin governance systems to reflect local conditions, and foster co-ordination between the different scales.
3. Encourage policy coherence through effective cross-sectoral co-ordination, especially between policies for water and the environment, health, energy, agriculture, industry, spatial planning and land use.
4. Adapt the level of capacity of responsible authorities to the complexity of water challenges to be met, and to the set of competencies required to carry out their duties.
5. Produce, update and share timely, consistent, comparable and policy-relevant water and water-related data and information, and use it to guide, assess and improve water policy.
6. Ensure that governance arrangements help mobilise water finance and allocate financial resources in an efficient, transparent and timely manner.
7. Ensure that sound water management regulatory frameworks are effectively implemented and enforced in pursuit of the public interest.
8. Promote the adoption and implementation of innovative water governance practices across responsible authorities, levels of government and relevant stakeholders.
9. Mainstream integrity and transparency practices across water policies, water institutions and water governance frameworks for greater accountability and trust in decision making.
10. Promote stakeholder engagement for informed and outcome-oriented contributions to water policy design and implementation.
11. Encourage water governance frameworks that help manage trade-offs across water users, rural and urban areas, and generations.
12. Promote regular monitoring and evaluation of water policy and governance where appropriate, share the results with the public and make adjustments when needed.

Source: OECD (2015), *OECD Principles on Water Governance*, www.oecd.org/gov/regional-policy/OECD-Principles-on-Water-Governance-brochure.pdf.

Putting the OECD Principles into practice

Since the Principles were adopted in 2015, they have been used for multiple purposes to guide decision makers and water practitioners on policy development and implementation, research and other forms of assessment or analyses of water governance gaps. The Principles have been applied across different scales, stakeholders and sectors, either as a tool to understand how water governance systems are performing at local, basin or national level, or as a reading template to guide decisions for water stakeholders and institutions on specific water functions (e.g. service delivery, water resources management, flood risk prevention, etc.). In January 2018, the journal *Water International* published a peer-reviewed set of articles reflecting such examples in its special issue "The OECD Principles on Water Governance: From Vision to Action". Some of these applications are summarised hereinafter and should neither be considered as the views of the authors of this report nor of the OECD.

Use of the Principles to assess water governance in six countries

Assessing whether policy and legal frameworks on water from around the world align with the OECD Principles was the aim of the study carried out by Neto et al. (2018). In particular, the authors conducted an analysis of six cases concerning national water policies from Australia, Brazil, New Zealand and South Africa, the European Union's Water Framework Directive and the Lisbon Charter on Water and Sanitation[3] (IWA, 2015). The paper did not compare the existing policy frameworks with each other, but rather their "performance" against the 12 OECD Principles. The analysis of what influences the implementation of the OECD Principles provided a basis for further recommendations, in relation to both water resources and water services. The authors assessed the cases against four criteria to obtain a diagnostic of the synergies, opportunities and constraints to implementation of the OECD Principles for each framework (Table 1.1). The criteria are: 1) alignment; 2) implementation; 3) on-ground results; 4) policy impacts. A Likert scale ranging from 1 (minimum) to 5 (maximum), utilising public information and expert opinions, was used to assess the implementation of the 12 OECD Principles for each of the cases. Table 1.1 summarises results by the three highest and three lowest scoring Principles. Results show that Principle 3 on policy coherence was one of the lowest scoring Principles against all four assessment criteria, while Principle 5 on data and information was one of the highest.

Table 1.1. **Highest and lowest scoring Principles against each of the criteria**

Criteria	Highest scoring Principle	Lowest scoring Principle
Alignment	Principle 2: Appropriate scales with basin systems Principle 10: Stakeholder engagement Principle 5: Data and information Principle 7: Regulatory frameworks	Principle 4: Capacity Principle 11: Trade-offs Principle 3: Policy coherence Principle 6: Financing
Implementation	Principle 7: Regulatory frameworks Principle 10: Stakeholder engagement Principle 5: Data and information	Principle 3: Policy coherence Principle 4: Capacity Principle 9: Integrity and transparency Principle 6: Financing Principle 8: Innovative governance
On-ground results	Principle 10: Stakeholder engagement Principle 5: Data and information Principle 12: Monitoring and engagement	Principle 3: Policy coherence Principle 6: Financing Principle 9: Integrity and transparency Principle 11: Trade-offs
Policy impact	Principle 10: Stakeholder engagement Principle 5: Data and information Principle 7: Regulatory frameworks	Principle 3: Policy coherence Principle 11: Trade-offs Principle 8: Innovative governance

Notes: Alignment: 1. No alignment; 2. Poor; 3. Moderate; 4. Good/strong; 5. Full alignment; Implementation: 1. No implementation; 2. Poor; 3. Moderate; 4. Good/strong; 5. Full implementation; On-ground results: 1. No evidence of change; 2. Poor; 3. Moderate; 4. Good/strong; 5. Major change evident; Policy impact: 1. No impact; 2. Poor; 3. Moderate; 4. Good/strong; 5. Very strong impact.

Source: Neto S. et al. (2018), "OECD Principles on Water Governance in Practice: An assessment of existing frameworks in Europe, Asia-Pacific, Africa and South America", https://doi.org/10.1080/02508060.2018.1402650.

Based on the assessment, the authors made recommendations for more effective implementation of the OECD Principles. These recommendations are clustered around the three dimensions of water governance: 1) improving "effectiveness", by reinforcing a comprehensive and holistic approach to water management and strengthening transboundary co-operation; 2) improving "efficiency", by filling the gap for weak national water policies and funding the whole water cycle; and 3) improving "trust and engagement", by networking around good practices and promoting national integrity and guidance with decisions devolved to the local level.

The study identified four main target areas for enhancing effectiveness, efficiency, and trust and engagement in water governance. In order of importance from the assessment, these were: policy coherence (Principle 3); financing (Principle 6); managing trade-offs across users, rural and urban areas, and generations (Principle 11); and integrity and transparency (Principle 9). To strengthen a comprehensive approach to water management, some Principles can be considered simultaneously (e.g. Principles 2, 3, 5, 9 and 11) in order to develop a clearer and broader understanding of the problems and the solutions. The paper concludes that the Principles are a good example of how the complexity of water problems demands holistic approaches and actions, including considerations of territorial, temporal and intergenerational continuity.

A framework to understand the evolution of water governance in France

Colon, Richard and Roche (2018) analysed the evolution of the French water governance system in light of the *OECD Principles on Water Governance*. Figure 1.4 shows a synthesis of how France has implemented each Principle since the 1960s. The authors claim that all of the Principles have been adopted and enforced at varying degrees.

The article emphasises that the French system has evolved during the last 50 years, but still needs to advance the implementation of certain OECD Principles. Water resource governance has made particular progress towards more effectiveness, more efficiency and higher levels of both trust and engagement (Principle 9), ensuring a sound water management regulatory framework (Principles 7) and promoting innovative water governance practices (Principle 8); managing water at appropriate scales (basin, catchment, administrative unit), fostering co-ordination between scales and promoting stakeholder engagement (basin committee, local water commission) (Principles 2 and 10); enhancing clear roles and responsibilities for water policy making and regulation (state), operational management (local authorities, contracting authorities, local water authorities), and public financing authorities (water agencies, local authorities) (Principles 1 and 6); enhancing data production and information, transparency (the National Agency for Water and Aquatic Environments [ONEMA], water agencies) (Principle 5); and encouraging regular monitoring and evaluation driven by European norms (Principle 12).

The authors' argue that the French water governance system has consistent institutional frameworks and tools, but challenges remain to encourage policy coherence and efficiency through more effective cross-sectoral co-ordination (Principle 3) and to adapt the level of capacity of responsible authorities regarding their new roles following the last territorial reform (Principle 4) (Figure 1.4). In terms of water resources management, the authors identify the need to develop a responsible, capable and empowered authority to manage flood risks, a topic which has gained particular traction with recent floods of the Seine River in Paris and elsewhere in France. In water and sanitation services, they noted the need to strengthen the capacity of responsible authorities to ensure the current level and quality of services, within a context of increasing uncertainties and lack of public finance.

Figure 1.4. **Colon, Richard and Roche's self-assessment of the implementation of the *OECD Principles on Water Governance* in France**

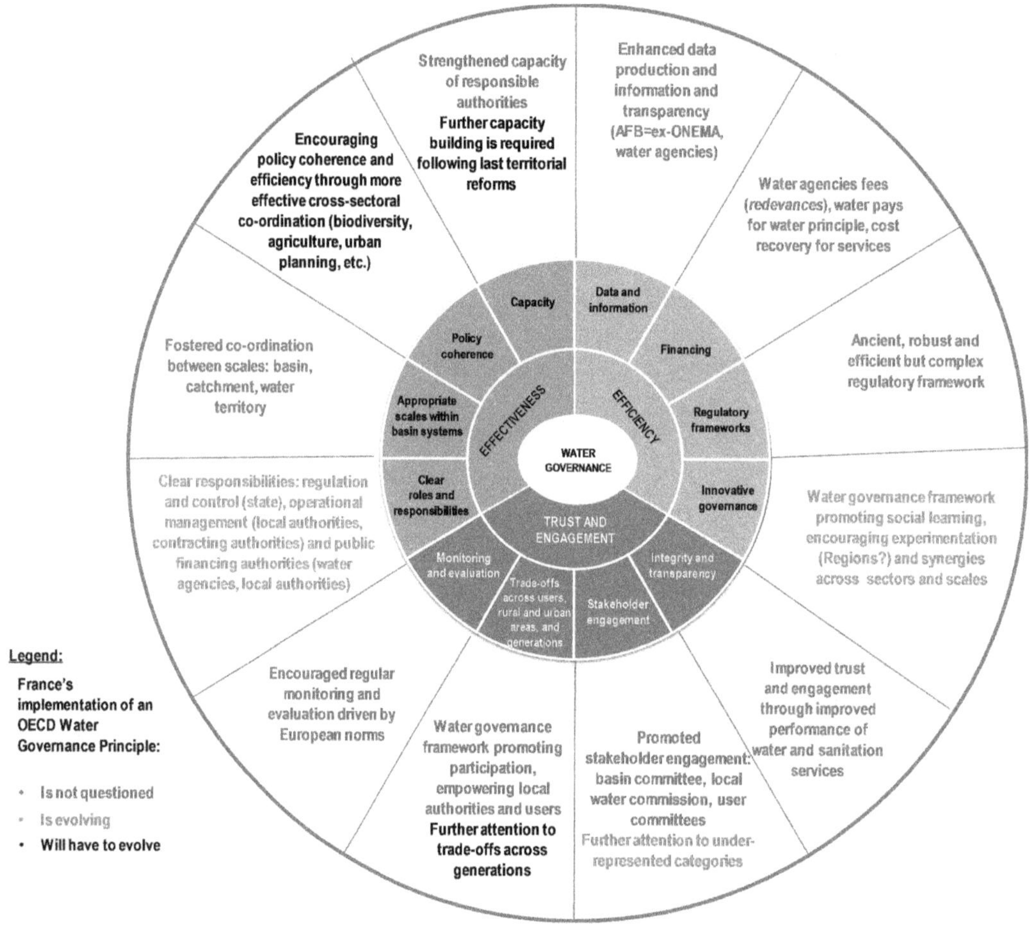

Source: Colon, M., S. Richard and P.A. Roche (2018), "The evolution of water governance in France from the 1960's: Disputes as major drivers for radical changes within a consensual framework", https://doi.org/10.1080/02508060.2018.1403013.

An application by the OECD of the Principles to water abstraction and pollution charges in Brazil

As part of a broader OECD/Brazil Policy dialogue carried out in 2016-17, the Principles were used as a reading template to understand governance challenges to the design and implementation of water abstraction and pollution charges in Brazil (OECD, 2017). Given that many countries are lagging behind in using economic instruments for water resources management, the case of Brazil provides useful lessons that can be considered in similar contexts. Currently, water charges are applied in six interstate river basins and six states in Brazil. However, there are several challenges in terms of institutional capacity, hydrological complexity and level of economic development, among others, which all affect the political choice of implementing water charges. Ultimately, strengthening water charges where they exist, and considering them where appropriate, could help to drive the necessary place-based actions to safeguard water quality and quantity (e.g. pollution and excessive abstraction) and to prevent water risks from becoming barriers to Brazil's sustainable growth now and in the future.

The report *Water Charges in Brazil: The Ways Forward* (OECD, 2017) considers that a perfect model for setting and governing water abstraction and pollution charges does not exist; however, based on international best practices it provides some ways forward to improve the current system. The OECD Principles can be a useful tool to assess whether some conditions are in place or not for economic instruments to achieve their economic and financial expected objectives (Table 1.2). In particular, there are two important features of a charging system that the Principles address: 1) the process of setting and enforcing charges, in particular, the modes of engaging with stakeholders matter; 2) the management of expenditure, since an essential part of the efficiency, effectiveness and political acceptability of a charging system is how revenues from water charges are spent.

According to the OECD Principles, water charges will only be viable if responsible authorities are clearly in charge and endowed with the needed capacity. They should be designed, collected and disbursed at the right scale; documented with robust information-based systems to guide decisions; driven by solid, realistic and policy-coherent planning; properly regulated with effective enforcement and compliance; engaged well upstream to raise their awareness and secure their buy-in; designed with a transparent implementation plan; and properly monitored and evaluated.

Two applications of the OECD Principles to the case of floods

Amidst a growing consensus that the frequency and number of people at risk from floods will increase in the future (OECD, 2012), flood risk governance, through which flood risk management is delivered, has emerged as a focal point of policy attention. In the pursuit of societal resilience, critical questions arise about how current governance arrangements support or constrain this goal. The pursuit of societal resilience and underlying discourses about efficiency and "doing better with less" have grown following the global financial crisis, and the associated increased need to demonstrate the best value for (public) money. Other standards of flood risk governance (and water governance at large), such as effectiveness, inclusiveness and trust (OECD, 2015), are important and allow for the application of the Principles to flood risks. Managing flood risks is a typical illustration of the shared responsibilities between public, private and non-profit actors and across levels of government, and of the need for place-based policies within national frameworks.

The Principles have been used as a reading grid to unpack the key features of flood risk governance approaches and to identify good practices across OECD countries. The results will be published in a forthcoming OECD working paper, "Managing 'too much water': A shared responsibility across cities, regions and countries. An application of the OECD Principles on Water Governance to the case of floods" (Akhmouch and Clavreul, forthcoming) that compiles a diverse group of 27 case studies in terms of:

- geographic location: Europe, Latin America, North America, Asia-Pacific, Africa
- management scale: national, regional/provincial/state, local, floodplain, river basin
- thematic focus: transboundary strategic plan for flood management; national policy and/or programmes; day-to-day management of floods in specific locations; state/provincial flood management plans; specific flood events; and research projects, at national or basin level.

Table 1.2. ***OECD Principles on Water Governance*** **applied to water charges in Brazil**

OECD Principle	Guidance for water abstraction and pollution charges in Brazil
Principle 1: Clear roles and responsibilities	– Clearly allocate and distinguish roles and responsibilities among federal, state and basin authorities for setting, implementing and regulating water charges, and adjust where need be based on results. – Identify and address duplications, overlaps, gaps or grey areas across levels of government, given the multiplicity of state and federal agencies involved. Overcome the legal gap concerning water agencies in charge of allocating revenues from water charges. – Ensure the consultative and deliberative functions of state/interstate river basin committees, and that state/national water councils are outcome-driven.
Principle 2: Appropriate scales within basin systems	– Design, collect and disburse water charges at the appropriate scale to reflect distinctive local capacity, hydrographic situations and water-related risks. – Foster co-ordination between hydrographic and administrative scales, which often do not correspond, with due attention to the higher complexity and multiplicity of stakeholders involved in federal rivers and the double dominion. – Foster co-ordination between local, state and federal levels of government.
Principle 3: Policy coherence	– Ensure that decisions taken in agriculture, energy, spatial planning, land use and environmental licensing do not undermine the water use efficiency rationale of charges. – Foster planning tools that drive water charges decisions and policy complementarity between water-related domains.
Principle 4: Capacity	– Identify and address capacity gaps to design and implement water charges in state/interstate river basin committees, agencies and councils.
Principle 5: Data and information	– Produce, update and share consistent and comparable data and information to guide, assess and improve the design and implementation of water charges. – Ground the level of charges on sound technical criteria, building on economic analysis to support decision making, and impacts on affordability and competitiveness.
Principle 6: Financing	– Ensure that governance arrangements help raise and spend revenues from water charges in an efficient, transparent and timely manner. – Ensure that the polluter-pays principle and user-pays principle are properly taken into account when designing charges. – Consider pros and cons of earmarking to show the benefits of water charges to end users (e.g. allowing them to access to some funds for water conservation measures).
Principle 7: Regulatory frameworks	– Ensure that regulatory frameworks support the efficiency, effectiveness and inclusiveness of water charges and are effectively implemented and enforced. – Ensure sound inspection and control mechanisms as well as sanctions and penalties in case of non-enforcement and compliance.
Principle 8: Innovative governance	– Promote innovative practices for the design and implementation of water charges (e.g. integrating behavioural dimensions into water charge design). – Enhance pilots and experimentation, building on the proposed OECD typology of states, to test some ways forward before upscaling.
Principle 9: Integrity and transparency	– Mainstream integrity and transparency practices in the water charge cycle, in particular: – who pays for what across water users – how revenues collected are spent and according to which criteria.
Principle 10: Stakeholder engagement	– Raise stakeholder awareness on water risks to secure the political/social buy-in for water charges. – Build capacity and share information for outcome-oriented debates and actions to charges in committees, councils and agencies. – Manage the risks of consultation capture, vested interests and low representation in deliberative and consultative fora.
Principle 11: Trade-offs across users, rural and urban areas, and generations	– Use water charges as a contribution to managing trade-offs across users, rural and urban areas, current and future generations. – Evaluate the possibility of cross-subsidies and solidarity mechanisms across users in period of droughts.
Principle 12: Monitoring and evaluation	– Promote regular monitoring and evaluation of the adequacy, implementation and results of water charges to assess to what extent they fulfil the intended outcomes and adapt where necessary.

Source: OECD (2017), *Water Charges in Brazil: The Ways Forward*, http://dx.doi.org/10.1787/9789264285712-en.

The paper also builds on the guidance provided by the OECD *Recommendation of the Council on the Governance of Critical Risks* and its applications to floods (OECD, 2014), which proposes overarching actions that governments at all levels can take to better assess, prevent, respond to and recover from the effects of extreme events, including floods. These experiences, together with discussions with flood practitioners, shed light on persistent challenges to making flood risk governance effective, efficient, inclusive and trustworthy, in particular:

- Greater effectiveness of flood risk governance will imply: 1) clarifying procedures and (legal) frameworks for the allocation of roles and responsibilities so as to solicit co-operation and avoid rivalry across institutions and levels of government; 2) strengthening the articulation of flood risk management plans elaborated at the national level, with the means of implementation and specific conditions at subnational level (i.e. regional/provincial, basin or local); 3) adopting mechanisms that can help manage multi-level dynamics inherent to flood risk management, and particularly between basin/sub-basins, upstream-downstream and sub-basin/ properties; 4) designing specific policies to entice sectoral coherence in flood risk management, with particular attention to nature/green infrastructure, climate change, territorial development and urban planning; 5) raising the awareness of decision makers on the need to assess capacity in flood risk management, and mobilise resources to bridge them; 6) building (technical and human) capacity among key stakeholders (e.g. farmers, water users' associations, etc.), so they can effectively take part in decision-making processes on flood risk management.
- Greater efficiency of flood risk governance will imply: 1) investing in long-term empirical data, including in historical flood events at finer levels; 2) improving databases, information and monitoring systems on flood risks, including by strengthening staff capacity to process data and increasing financial resources for maintenance; 3) securing perennial and innovative financing, relying on cost-benefit analyses that include ecosystems services and not only market value; 4) reducing the administrative burden of flood-related regulatory processes.
- Greater inclusiveness and trust in flood risk governance will imply: 1) strengthening enforcement mechanisms for integrity and transparency, including codes of conduct related to open data and the protection of intellectual property rights; 2) providing institutional support to stakeholder engagement (e.g. clear procedures and commitments, resources, information sharing, etc.); 3) adopting compensation measures to address trade-offs based on an understanding of where the balance between costs and benefits allows the most outcomes; 4) developing reporting processes to monitor flood risk governance arrangements, and loop monitoring outcomes in policy making and implementation.

A group of Dutch stakeholders also used the OECD Principles to assess the Dutch Flood Protection Programme in the Netherlands (Seijger et al., 2018). The paper explores the practical value of the Principles in assessing water governance practices through a survey to respondents on how the Flood Protection Programme performed. The survey was distributed to ten key professionals working in the Flood Protection Programme and was completed by five groups of experts (at a 50% response rate). Figure 1.5 depicts the extent to which survey respondents considered the programme to perform in accordance with the Principles. The programme achieved four Principles "well" (6, 7, 8 and 9); three "fairly" (1, 7, 2) and six "partly" (5, 3, 4, 10, 11 and 12). Although, Principle 12 (monitoring and evaluation) was considered partly achieved, it was also perceived as difficult to assess by the respondents.

Figure 1.5. **Seijger et al. self-assessment of the Dutch Flood Protection Programme against the *OECD Principles on Water Governance***

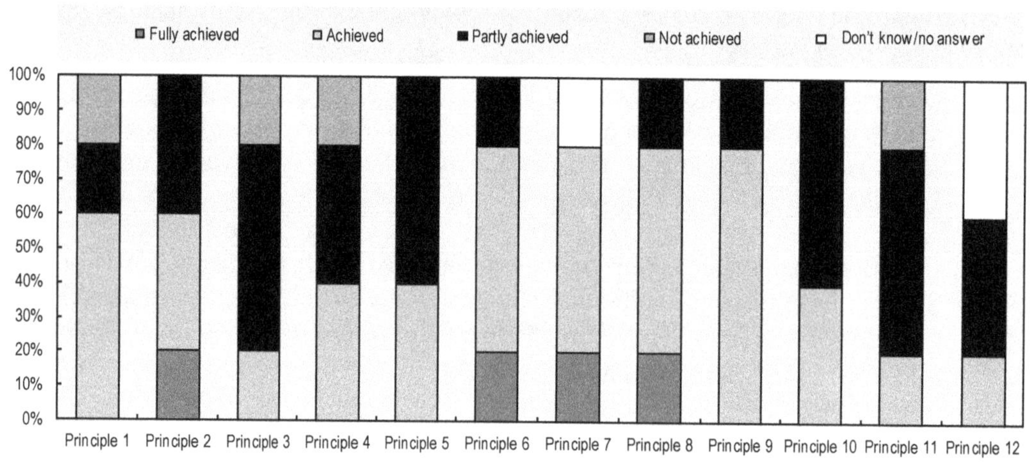

Source: Seijger, C. et al. (2018) "Functions of OECD water governance principles in assessing water governance practices: Assessing the Dutch Flood Protection Programme", https://doi.org/10.1080/02508060.2018.1402607.

The analysis revealed various functions of the OECD Principles, from enhancing understanding and reforming the agenda to reflecting and taking informed action. In particular, it revealed how the Principles had practical value in generating lessons to strengthen the effectiveness, efficiency and legitimacy of the Dutch Flood Protection Programme. In addition, the assessment revealed functions of the *OECD Principles on Water Governance* in enabling and stimulating learning to strengthen a water governance system. These functions are to: enhance the understanding of the water governance system; reform the agenda; reflect and set priorities; inform action. Recommendations are given on how the OECD Principles can be used to come to meaningful action-oriented water governance assessments, including contextualisation, multiple methods, inclusiveness and periodical assessments.

An OECD application of the Principles to monitoring and evaluation of groundwater

The OECD also used the Principles to identify the characteristics of a monitoring and evaluation framework for groundwater governance (Akhmouch and Clavreul, 2017). The book chapter argues that measuring whether or not certain conditions are in place is the first crucial step to identifying what can hinder effective groundwater policy design and implementation (e.g. roles and responsibilities are unclear or overlapping), what is missing (e.g. lack of or insufficient co-ordination with other policy fields such as agriculture or land use) and what can be improved (e.g. tools for collective groundwater management). Thus, it suggests 12 mutually reinforcing and complementary components that can provide a framework of reference and be tailored to local contexts (Table 1.3).

Table 1.3. **Monitoring and evaluating groundwater through the *OECD Principles on Water Governance***

OECD Principle	Action
Principle 1: Clear roles and responsibilities	Monitoring and evaluating groundwater governance should begin by considering whether roles and responsibilities for groundwater policy making, policy implementation, operational management and regulation are clearly allocated.
Principle 2: Appropriate scales within basin systems	The monitoring and evaluation framework should investigate whether groundwater policies are fitted to places and take account of multi-level dynamics across the national, federal/state, basin and local levels, and whether there are co-ordination challenges between the different scales.
Principle 3: Policy coherence	The monitoring and evaluation framework should gauge groundwater governance by looking at its close relationship with various sectoral policies, such as agriculture and land use. It should also look into the complementarities between groundwater and surface water policies when these are devised separately.
Principle 4: Capacity	The monitoring and evaluation framework should assess whether the needed capacities, both technical and non-technical, are secured to shoulder responsibilities for groundwater management.
Principle 5: Data and information	The monitoring and evaluation framework should determine whether data and information are produced, updated and shared, in a timely and policy-relevant manner.
Principle 6: Financing	The monitoring and evaluation framework should investigate whether the performance of groundwater management agencies has been impaired by shortages of finance, and identify where investment needs are most pressing in groundwater governance to ensure that fundamental functions of regulation, planning and monitoring are not under-resourced. It would also help identify where better governance can contribute to efficiency gains across the groundwater chain, for example through improved collaboration between authorities and pooling of financial resources and capacities at the relevant scale for optimising resources.
Principle 7: Regulatory frameworks	The monitoring and evaluation framework for groundwater governance should promote formal, legally binding documents applicable to groundwater that include the Principles necessary to achieve sustainable groundwater governance. The framework should diagnose whether such regulatory texts include: 1) a common terminology that is rooted either in the state-of-the-art hydrogeology or legal norms, as appropriate; 2) definitions and scope that recognise the duality of groundwater being both part of and apart from the contemporary hydrologic cycle, thus including aquifers of all types whether non-recharging, layered or linked to surface water; 3) norms presently under-represented in legally binding texts. Groundwater laws should also be coherent with land laws that have important implications for access to groundwater and its protection.
Principle 8: Innovative governance	The monitoring and evaluation framework for groundwater governance should assess whether the enabling environment is in place for innovative approaches (e.g. identifying barriers to and mechanisms for innovation). The overall objective should be to transform groundwater governance so it is fit for future challenges.
Principle 9: Integrity and transparency	The monitoring and evaluation framework should diagnose what makes the breeding ground for corruption in groundwater governance, and promote enhanced understanding of groundwater constraints and vulnerabilities among all stakeholders, and information transparency through open access to data on groundwater resource and quality status, and water well abstraction licenses. It should also foster accountability of decision makers and stakeholders as regards the way they manage, access and use groundwater resources (e.g. procurement processes for irrigation systems) by calling for codes of conduct and charters.
Principle 10: Stakeholder engagement	The monitoring and evaluation framework for groundwater governance should help identify the wide range of stakeholders concerned with groundwater policy making and implementation (including an inventory of groundwater users and uses), as well as check whether the appropriate mechanisms are in place for stakeholder engagement.
Principle 11: Trade-offs across users, rural and urban areas, and generations	The monitoring and evaluation framework for groundwater governance should look into the main trade-offs relating to groundwater management and measure their distributional consequences on users and places. It should also assess whether mechanisms are in place to address these trade-offs.
Principle 12: Monitoring and evaluation	The monitoring and evaluation framework for groundwater governance should instil a culture of assessment and accountability when it comes to groundwater policy choices and their implementation. It should review whether dedicated institutions are charged with monitoring and evaluation responsibilities, and whether they make the results of their assessments transparent.

Source: Adapted from Akhmouch A. and D. Clavreul (2017), "Assessing and monitoring groundwater governance".

An appraisal of institutional development and social learning through the OECD Principles

Menard, Jimenez and Tropp (2018) review sources of misalignment between the institutional arrangements, the incentives and the resources mobilised in water policies. The paper investigates the gaps that pertain to policy formulation, policy operationalisation, characteristics and behaviour of stakeholders, and to the over-arching institutional environment in which these gaps are embedded. It suggests that the Principles make an important step in addressing the policy gaps identified by taking on board the institutional settings and the diverse modalities of governance they command. The *OECD Principles on Water Governance*, rather than providing a general toolkit unfit for most situations, deliver and widely diffuse recommendations to policy makers to consider when reviewing existing policies or defining new ones (Table 1.4).

The paper argues that the institutional environment is not necessarily defined at the national level: it can be associated to supranational or regional power and in many cases to transboundary water entities setting the rules. Moreover, rules are not necessarily embedded in laws: in many countries, they are rooted in customary water rights. However, there is an institutional layer (meso-institutions), which is often either neglected or even missing, and that links the macro-institutional layer at which rules are defined and the micro-institutional layer at which implementation takes place. The combination of institutions (regulatory agencies, public bureaus, local commissions, stakeholder committees) and mechanisms (administrative rules or protocols) defines different meso-institutions and makes them a central piece to understand and explain policy implementation gaps. This intermediate layer is underlying many of the Principles enunciated in the *OECD Principles on Water Governance*.

The authors state that be able to achieve upward and downward accountability and to reach non-discriminatory outcomes, meso-institutions need to be designed (or reformed) in a way that improves integrity, transparency and participation (Principle 9). Implementing reliable institutional procedures to monitor and evaluate policies adopted (Principle 12) is essential to build legitimacy for the policies chosen and to avoid increasing gaps that can undermine efforts to provide universal access to safe drinkable water at sustainable economic and political transaction costs. It is also key to the preservation of the resource, an aspect that may not be emphasised enough in the existing version of the Principles.

Another article has devoted specific attention to the topic of stakeholder engagement as featured under Principle 10 (Wehn et al., 2018). The paper argues that a reframing of stakeholder engagement as a process of social learning opens up more possibilities than just participation, as it carries an explicit purpose which underpins design and process considerations. It also opens up discussion on the responsibilities of those involved as initiators, designers, facilitators, participants and "recipients" of the process. If no changes are likely, due to prohibitive institutional arrangements, for example, then inviting stakeholders into a process predicated on social learning and dialogue is ethically questionable. It follows that while designers and facilitators cannot be held accountable if the stakeholder engagement "fails" in terms of social learning, they are responsible for ensuring that the enabling conditions for social learning are met.

Table 1.4. **Type of gaps in policy implementation, and typical causes**

Policy implementation gap	Causes	Link to *OECD Principles on Water Governance*
Gaps in policy formulation process	– Lack of national oversight over policy formulation – External pressure to adopt blue print policies not adapted to the context – Lack of high-level political commitment – Lack of participation in policy formulation – Policy capture by elites or influential groups	– Principle 1: Clearly allocate and distinguish roles and responsibilities for water policy making, policy implementation, operational management and regulation, and foster co-ordination across these responsible authorities – Principle 4: Adapt the level of capacity of responsible authorities to the complexity of the water challenges to be met, and to the set of competencies required to carry out their duties – Principle 10: Promote stakeholder engagement for informed and outcome-oriented contributions to water policy design and implementation
Gaps in operationalisation of the policy	– Mismatch between the responsibilities and resources – Time needed to build capacity not adequately considered – Lack of legitimacy of institutions that implement policy – Misalignment between water policies and informal water institutions – Lack of capacity to monitor and enforce agreed norms – No channels to signal users' demands or express dissatisfaction	– Principle 1: Institutional roles and responsibilities (see above) – Principle 4: Capacity (see above) – Principle 6: Ensure that governance arrangements help mobilise water finance and allocate financial resources in an efficient, transparent and timely manner – Principle 7: Ensure that sound water management regulatory frameworks are effectively implemented and enforced in pursuit of the public interest – Principle 9: Mainstream integrity and transparency practices across water policies, water institutions and water governance frameworks for greater accountability and trust in decision making – Principle 12: Promote regular monitoring and evaluation of water policy and governance where appropriate, share the results with the public and make adjustments when needed
Gaps related to characteristics and behaviour of stakeholders	– Monopolistic position of providers – Third-party opportunism – Quality of the representation of stakeholders – Capture of stakeholder representation by specific interest groups – Corruption	– Principle 9: Integrity and transparency (see above) – Principle 10: Stakeholder engagement (see above) – Principle 4: Capacity (see above)
Gaps related to the overarching country governance situation	– Political instability, protracted crisis and insecurity – Government's lack of capacity to conduct basic functions – Lack of accountability in the public sector – Poor top-down discipline in government – No practice of democratic culture, including debate, consultation and participation	– Principle 7: Regulation (see above) – Principle 3: Encourage policy coherence through effective cross-sectoral co-ordination, especially between policies for water and the environment, health, energy, agriculture, industry, spatial planning and land use

Source: Menard, C., A. Jimenez and H. Tropp (2018), "Addressing the policy implementation gaps in water services: The key role of meso-institutions", https://doi.org/10.1080/02508060.2017.1405696.

A survey taking stock of the use and dissemination of the OECD Principles

An online survey carried out between 15 and 24 January 2018 collected inputs on: 1) the use of the OECD Principles, in particular on how they guide and inform activities and practices; 2) to what extent and how the OECD Principles have been disseminated; 3) perceived needs for improving the uptake and dissemination of the OECD Principles.

The survey targeted the members of the OECD Water Governance Initiative and the broader Global Coalition for Good Water Governance, a platform gathering 170 stakeholder groups, including 35 OECD countries and 7 non-OECD economies that have endorsed the Principles. The members of the Global Coalition for Good Water Governance committed to: use the Principles to guide their activities and practices; disseminate the Principles to their constituencies, members, partners and networks; report back on the above to help the OECD Secretariat assess the use and dissemination of the Principles.

In total, 85 answers (50% response rate) were received from over 30 countries (25 OECD countries and 5 non-OECD economies) and different sectors, including private companies, service providers, civil society, governments, academia, international organisations, water-user organisations, etc. (see Annex 1.A1).

Use of the OECD Principles to guide activities and practices

A majority of the respondents have used the Principles to take decisions, make water policy choices or plan programmatic activities. In fact, 80% of the respondents reported that they have used the Principles "often" or "sometimes" (Figure 1.6) in these contexts. The overall results suggest that organisations that have endorsed the Principles and committed to their implementation have widely used them for multiple purposes. In this respect, 54% of the respondents (Figure 1.7) have used the Principles to identify water governance practices that could guide their decision making. A large number of respondents have used the Principles as a tool for assessing water governance in a particular context or to engage in a policy dialogue with relevant stakeholders within or outside of their country (42% and 41%, respectively). The Principles were also included in advocacy and awareness-raising campaigns, guides for policy processes and practices, and various capacity development and educational materials (39%, 35% and 34%, respectively). Lastly, one-quarter of the respondents has used the Principles to guide strategic orientations and practices of their own organisations.

Respondents provided concrete examples on how they had used the Principles and what they had learnt from them:

- **Multi-stakeholder dialogue.** Some respondents referred to the Principles as a "learning tool" that can be used in discussions and dialogues with a large variety of stakeholders, including national environmental agencies, regulators or local stakeholders. It was also pointed out that the Principles can encourage improvements in the way stakeholders are engaged in the decision-making process. For instance, in the Amu Darya River Basin (Central Asia), the OECD Principles were used for more active and informed stakeholder engagement to improve transboundary water management and adaptation to climate change. In Peru, the National Water Agency conducted 1 national and 14 regional multi-stakeholder workshops to build consensus on the water governance challenges faced by the country and the ways forward to address them.

Figure 1.6. **Frequency in using the *OECD Principles on Water Governance* to guide activities and practices**

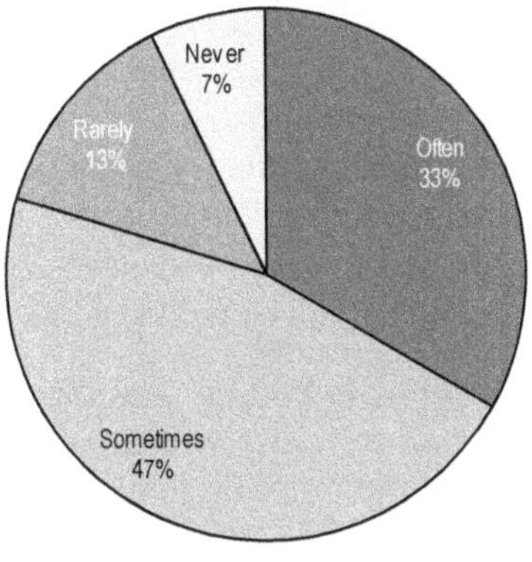

Source: Based on the 85 responses to the survey on the use and dissemination of the *OECD Principles on Water Governance* (15-24 January 2018).

Figure 1.7. **Activities making use of the *OECD Principles on Water Governance***

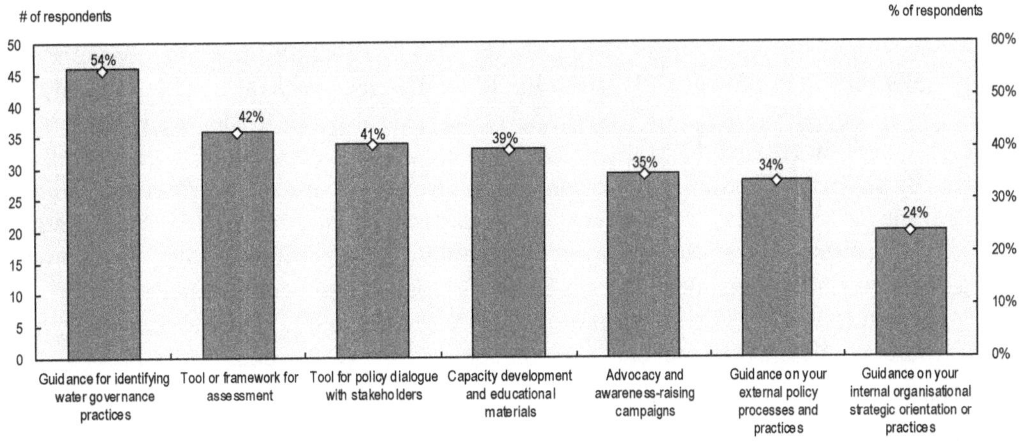

Notes: "Tool or framework for assessment" relates to assessing water governance status or progress of a particular context and scale; "capacity development and educational materials" relates to including the Principles in capacity development and educational materials, handbooks, manuals.

Source: Based on the 85 responses to the survey on the use and dissemination of the *OECD Principles on Water Governance* (15-24 January 2018).

- **Assess water governance status at various scales.** For instance, the Principles were used as an analytical framework for evaluating water governance in Norway during 2010-15. In particular, they helped identify critical issues of the governance system and served as a checklist to propose improvements in the water sector. A respondent had also used the Principles to assess current policies in flood risk management. Another respondent stated that the Principles helped introduce into their assessment governance aspects that were previously overlooked (in terms of inclusiveness, competitiveness and transparency). The Principles have been also claimed to be a dynamic tool that allows for reflection on water governance and can contribute to implement changes.

- **Capacity development, education and research.** For example, the Network of Asian River Basin Organizations introduced the Principles into integrated water resources management implementation handbook guidance to assess river basin organisation performance and conduct benchmarking. Moreover, the Principles, along with some OECD reports, have been used in academic graduate programmes on water governance as well as for research activities, the development of specific capacity-building tools and to explore new research topics. In general, respondents claimed that the Principles are easy to understand and help raise awareness among non-expert audiences on the challenges faced by the water sector.
- **Guidance to internal and external processes and practices.** A respondent mentioned that in his/her country, the public administration is using the Principles to guide the role, responsibilities and functions of the new national water resource management agency. Several respondents also reported having extensive references to the Principles in international conferences, in dialogues to identify good practices and pitfalls to avoid, to reinforce the message of governance as a means to improve policy outcomes, and to foster the implementation of water policies at the right geographic scale. One organisation claimed that the Principles are being used to mainstream and improve transparency, public participation and communication practices in their daily activities.

A majority of the respondents have used the OECD Principles both as a package and individually (46%), while only 28% used the Principles as a package, and 26% used only some of the Principles (Figure 1.8). From the survey, it is difficult to identify whether some Principles were more used than others, as they were applied depending on the purpose of the activity and usefulness in specific contexts. For instance, a respondent claimed that in Portugal the "effectiveness" (Principles 1-4) pillar is relevant, particularly when looking back at the institutional reform of the water governance system in the country. A network of basin organisations claimed that given the scope of their activities, Principles 2, 4 and 10 related to managing water at the right scale, the capacity of responsible authorities to face water challenges and stakeholder engagement, received special attention.

Finally, only 7% of respondents (6 out of 54) reported having never used the Principles. The low rate of responses does not allow for a thorough assessment of "why" these organisations did not use of the Principles. However, several reasons were reported, including poor understanding of the Principles within their organisation; encountering capacity challenges related to staff, time or funding; weak alignment of the Principles with their organisational priorities; and prior implementation of the Principles in the respondent's country of residence.

Dissemination of the OECD Principles

A qualified majority of the respondents claimed that they have disseminated the Principles often or sometimes (78%; Figure 1.9). Mirroring the results of frequency of usage, only 21% have "rarely" disseminated the Principles and 1% claims they have "never" disseminated them. In 77% of the cases, dissemination occurs by referencing the Principles in workshops, meetings or seminars, and in 63% of the cases by using them in reports or other types of publications. The Principles are also disseminated through newsletters and news updates (39%), by including information on the Principles on the respondents' own websites (20%), and through social media channels, such as Twitter, LinkedIn, etc. (19%; Figure 1.10).

Figure 1.8. **Modality of use of the *OECD Principles on Water Governance***

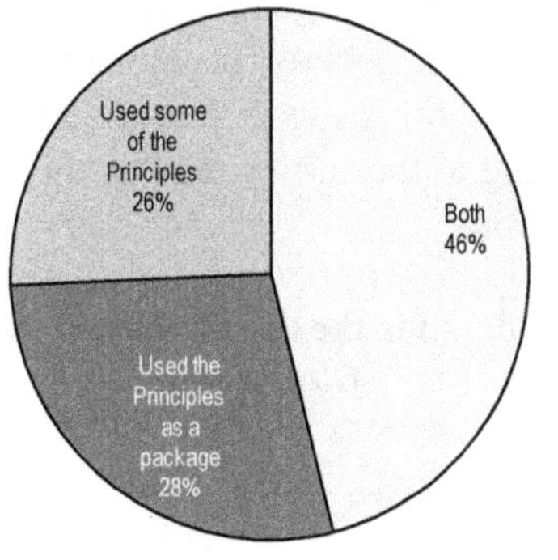

Source: Based on the 85 responses to the survey on the use and dissemination of the *OECD Principles on Water Governance* (15-24 January 2018).

Figure 1.9. **Frequency of dissemination of the *OECD Principles on Water Governance***

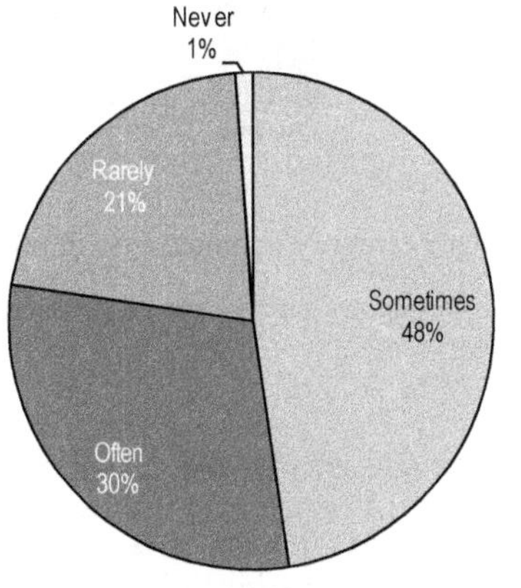

Source: Based on the 85 responses to the Survey on the use and dissemination of the *OECD Principles on Water Governance* (15-24 January 2018).

Figure 1.10. **Communication channels to disseminate the *OECD Principles on Water Governance***

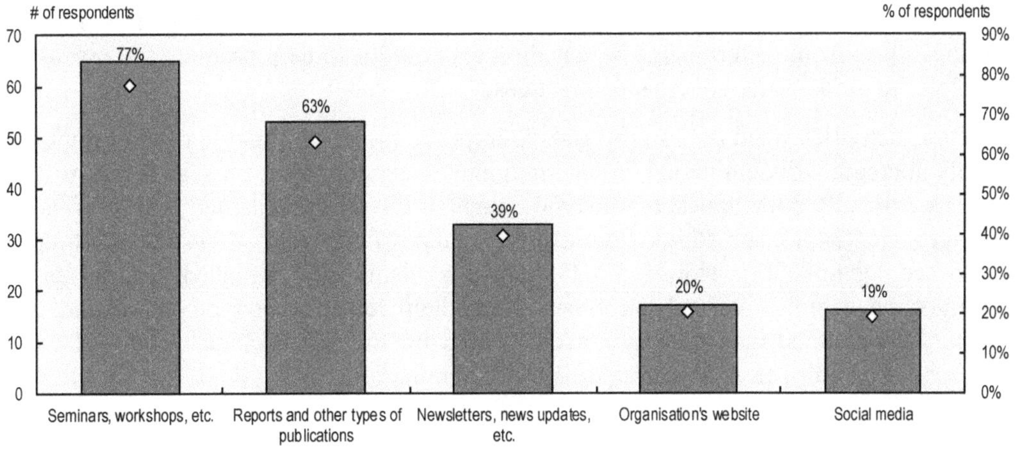

Source: Based on the 85 responses to the survey on the use and dissemination of the *OECD Principles on Water Governance* (15-24 January 2018).

The Principles are disseminated to a fairly broad group of constituencies (Figure 1.11). Governments (66%) and other public agencies (64%) were the most targeted group, followed by academia (51%), civil society organisations (48%), and international and multilateral organisations (39%), the private sector (31%), and financial institutions or bilateral donors (19%). According to the survey results, the Principles were also disseminated widely among youth organisations.

Figure 1.11. **Targeted stakeholders for the dissemination of the *OECD Principles on Water Governance***

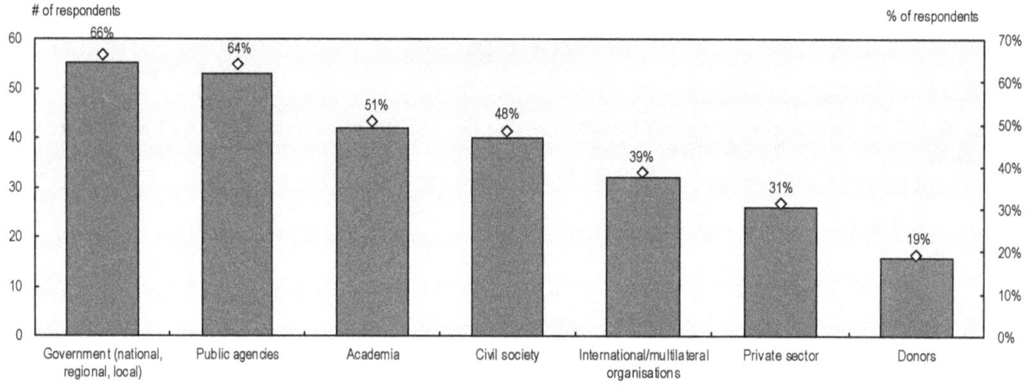

Note: "Public agencies" stands for regulators, water committees, water utilities, basin organisations, etc.

Source: Based on the 85 responses to the survey on the use and dissemination of the *OECD Principles on Water Governance* (15-24 January 2018).

Perceived needs to make better use of the OECD Principles

Linking the Principles to global agendas such as the Sustainable Development Goals, the Paris Agreement and Habitat III was highlighted as the most prominent activity to increase their use (67% of responses) (Figure 1.12). Another important group of responses (44%) pointed out the need to develop more tools that promote the use of the Principles, which is closely related to the 39% that indicated that capacity development activities on how to apply the Principles as a tool for dialogues and assessments, among others, would help increase their use. Another 38% saw a need for raising awareness about the content and relevance of the Principles. Lastly, 36% of the responses believed that incentives from governments or stakeholders could also help promote the use of the Principles to guide water governance practices.

Three activities stand out as proposals to improve the dissemination of the Principles, namely increased dissemination in international water-related events and fora (60%); more user-friendly communication materials, such as virtual tutorials, targeted information packages, etc. (54%); and ad hoc trainings for public officials and interested stakeholders (51%; see Figure 1.13). However, 31% of respondents also signalled that increasing dissemination in non-water related events could help reach other type of stakeholders. Lastly, 26% claimed that there is a need to increase the use of social media (Twitter, Facebook, LinkedIn, etc.), as useful tools for dissemination.

Figure 1.12. **Proposals to make better use of the *OECD Principles on Water Governance***

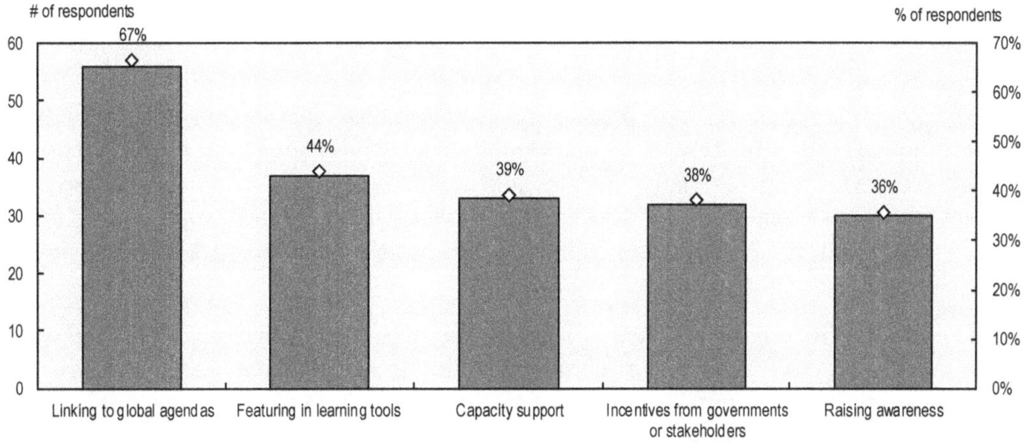

Notes: "Tools for learning" relates to guidance documents, handbooks, virtual tutorials, webinars, videos, etc.; "capacity support for using the Principles" relates to using them as a basis for water policy dialogues, assessments, identifying evolving practices, etc. (e.g. through training of trainers); "incentives from governments" relates to, for example, creating conditionalities in technical assistance programmes, financial support to organise dialogues around the Principles, etc.

Source: Based on the 85 responses to the survey on the use and dissemination of the *OECD Principles on Water Governance* (15-24 January 2018).

Figure 1.13. **Proposals to improve the dissemination of the *OECD Principles on Water Governance***

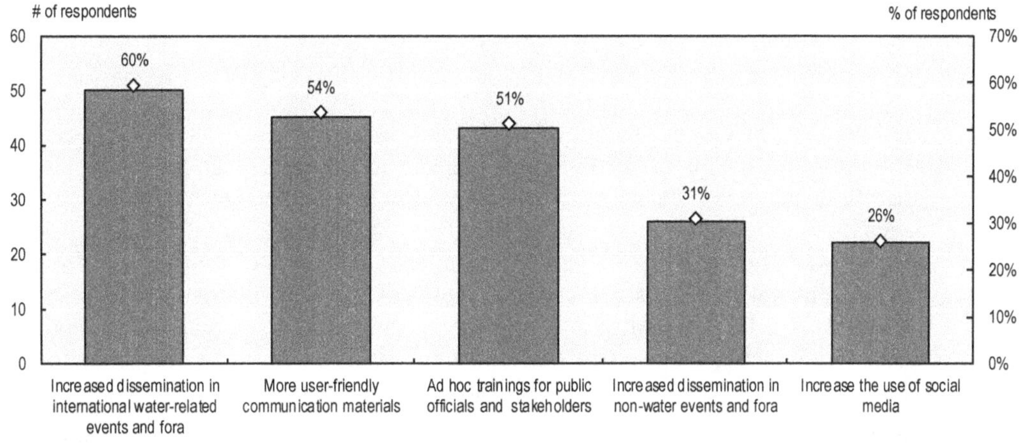

Source: Based on the 85 responses to the survey on the use and dissemination of the *OECD Principles on Water Governance* (15-24 January 2018).

An implementation framework to support the use of the Principles

The improvement of governance will be important to enhance water security while coping with water challenges now and in the future. It leads to reduced transaction costs and to economic savings, and has positive welfare effects on social and environmental well-being and sustained economic growth. Meeting water challenges by improving governance is one important key to meeting internationally agreed development goals and targets such as the SDGs or the Paris Agreement. The OECD Principles were developed in their own right to respond to water challenges in interested countries, cities and regions, but they can also be used as a robust and comprehensive framework and source of inspiration to engage a multi-stakeholder dialogue on the achievement of other water-related global agendas.

The Principles are used in multiple ways across scales and sectors. They have been helpful in providing a framework to understand water governance systems, to determine if they are performing optimally, and to help institute changes in policy and practice whenever deemed required. In addition, they have helped to promote stakeholder inclusiveness and engagement and pointed to gains in effectiveness and efficiency in water decision making.

The Water Governance Indicator Framework (Chapter 2) and the evolving water governance practices (Chapter 3) are implementation tools that have been developed as a means to support further uptake and use of the Principles in interested cities, regions and countries. They are part of a broader menu of options to guide dialogue across stakeholders on the performance of water governance systems. The OECD Water Governance Indicator Framework is intended as a self-assessment tool, to evaluate the current water governance situation and expected changes in a participative manner while the identified evolving water governance practices seek to promote bench-learning and scale-up suitable practices.

Notes

1. The Regional Development Policy Committee was created in 1999 with the goal of identifying the nature of territorial challenges and assisting governments in the assessment and improvement of their territorial policies. Through its mandate today, the committee aims to serve as the premier international forum for senior-level policy makers to identify, discuss, develop and disseminate a vision of regional development policy that is place-based, multi-level, multi-sectoral, evidence-based and innovative. The committee also seeks to enhance well-being and living standards in all region types, from cities to rural areas, and improve their contribution to national performance and more inclusive and resilient societies.

2. The Global Coalition for Good Water Governance is composed of more than 170 members from government, and public, private and non-governmental organisations. Members have endorsed the principles and committed to contribute to their implementation and dissemination. More information is available at: https://www.oecd.org/cfe/regional-policy/Global-Coalition-Good-Water-Governance-Flyer.pdf.

3. The Lisbon Charter is an international framework of good practice for public policy and regulation in drinking water supply, sanitation and wastewater management services; the text was agreed by over 200 delegates from 56 different countries, and approved by the IWA General Assembly in 2015.

References

Akhmouch, A. and D. Clavreul (forthcoming), "Managing 'too much water': A shared responsibility across cities, regions and countries. An application of the OECD Principles on Water Governance to the case of floods", OECD Working Paper, OECD Publishing, Paris, forthcoming.

Akhmouch A. and D. Clavreul (2017), "Assessing and monitoring groundwater governance", in: Villholth, K. et al. (eds.), *Advances in Groundwater Governance*, CRC Press, London.

Colon, M., S. Richard and P.A. Roche (2018), "The evolution of water governance in France from the 1960's: Disputes as major drivers for radical changes within a consensual framework", *Water International*, Vol. 43/1: The OECD Principles on Water Governance: From Policy Standards to Practice, pp. 109-132, https://doi.org/10.1080/02508060.2018.1403013.

IWA (2015), "The Lisbon Charter: Guiding the public policy and regulation of drinking water supply, sanitation and wastewater management services", International Water Association, London, www.iwa-network.org/publications/the-lisbon-charter.

Menard, C., A. Jimenez and H. Tropp (2018), "Addressing the policy implementation gaps in water services: The key role of meso-institutions", *Water International*, Vol. 43/1: The OECD Principles on Water Governance: From Policy Standards to Practice, pp. 13-33, https://doi.org/10.1080/02508060.2017.1405696.

Neto, S. et al. (2018), "OECD Principles on Water Governance in practice: An assessment of existing frameworks in Europe, Asia-Pacific, Africa and South America", *Water International*, Vol. 43/1: The OECD Principles on Water Governance: From Policy Standards to Practice, pp. 60-89, https://doi.org/10.1080/02508060.2018.1402650.

OECD (2017), *Water Charges in Brazil: The Ways Forward*, OECD Publishing, Paris, http://dx.doi.org/10.1787/9789264285712-en.

OECD (2016), "OECD Water Governance Initiative: Terms of reference 2016-18", GOV/RDPC(2016)2, OECD, Paris.

OECD (2015), *OECD Principles on Water Governance*, OECD, Paris, www.oecd.org/gov/regional-policy/OECD-Principles-on-Water-Governance-brochure.pdf.

OECD (2014), *Recommendation of the Council on the Governance of Critical Risks*, OECD, Paris, https://www.oecd.org/mcm/C-MIN(2014)8-ENG.pdf.

OECD (2012), *OECD Environmental Outlook to 2050*, OECD Publishing, Paris, http://dx.doi.org/10.1787/9789264122246-en.

OECD (2011), *Water Governance in OECD Countries: A Multi-level Approach*, OECD Publishing, Paris, http://dx.doi.org/10.1787/9789264119284-en.

Sadoff, C.W. et al. (2015), *Securing Water, Sustaining Growth: Report of the GWP/OECD Task Force on Water Security and Sustainable Growth*, University of Oxford, Oxford, United Kingdom, https://www.water.ox.ac.uk/wp-content/uploads/2015/04/SCHOOL-OF-GEOGRAPHY-SECURING-WATER-SUSTAINING-GROWTH-DOWNLOADABLE.pdf.

Seijger, C. et al. (2018), "Functions of OECD water governance principles in assessing water governance practices: Assessing the Dutch Flood Protection Programme", *Water International*, Vol. 43/1: The OECD Principles on Water Governance: From Policy Standards to Practice, pp. 90-108, https://doi.org/10.1080/02508060.2018.1402607.

When, U. et al. (2018), "Stakeholder engagement in water governance as social learning: Lessons from practice", *Water International*, Vol. 43/1: The OECD Principles on Water Governance: From Policy Standards to Practice, pp. 34-59, https://doi.org/10.1080/02508060.2018.1403083.

World Economic Forum (2018), *The Global Risks Report 2018*, 13th Edition, World Economic Forum, Geneva, www3.weforum.org/docs/WEF_GRR18_Report.pdf.

Annex 1.A1.

Respondents to the survey on the use and dissemination of the *OECD Principles on Water Governance*

Table 1.A1.1. **Respondents to the survey on the use and dissemination of the *OECD Principles on Water Governance***

Organisation	Area/detail
Network of Asian River Basin Organizations (NARBO)	Asia
Australian National University (ANU)	Australia
Association of Gas & Water (ÖVGW)	Austria
Association of Public Services and Public Enterprises (VÖWG)	Austria
Federal Ministry for Sustainability and Tourism	Austria
EurEau	Belgium
Flanders Knowledge Center Water (Vlakwa/VITO)	Belgium
Protos (development co-operation NGO)	Belgium
Ministry of Agriculture	Czech Republic
Permanent Delegation of the Czech Republic to the OECD	Czech Republic
Environmental Protection Agency	Denmark
European Irrigation Association (EIA)	Europe
Aalto University – Water and Development Research Group	Finland
AgroParisTech	France
Centre National de la Recherche Scientifique (CNRS)	France
Eau de Paris	France
FP2E	France
Scientific and Technical Association for Water and the Environment (ASTEE)	France
University of Paris (Pantheon-Sorbonne)	France
Water Solidarity Programme (pS-Eau)	France
Water Youth Network	France
Association of Energy and Water Industries (BDEW)	Germany
Federal Ministry for Economic Co-operation and Development (BMZ)	Germany
Banka BioLoo	India
Peter Gammeltoft	Independent expert
Aqua Publica Europea	International
AquaFed – The International Federation of Private Water Operators	International
SUEZ	International
The International Water Association (IWA)	International
Transparency International	International
Veolia	International
Water Integrity Network (WIN)	International
World Water Council (WWC)	International
Israel Water Authority	Israel
Metropolitana Milanese (MM Spa)	Italy
Regulatory Agency for Energy, Networks and Environment (ARERA)	Italy
Korea Environment Institute	Korea
Global Water Partnership – Mediterranean (GWP-Med)	Mediterranean region
Mediterranean Institute for Water/Institut Méditerranéen de l'Eau (IME)	Mediterranean region
National Association of Water and Sanitation Utilities (ANEAS)	Mexico
National Water Commission (CONAGUA)	Mexico
State Water Commission of Queretaro	Mexico
Deltares	Netherlands

Table 1.A1.1. **Respondents to the survey on the use and dissemination of the *OECD Principles on Water Governance*** (*continued*)

Organisation	Area/detail
IHE Delft Institute for Water Education	Netherlands
Ministry of Infrastructure and Water Management	Netherlands
University of Utrecht	Netherlands
University of Utrecht – Centre for Water, Oceans and Sustainability Law (UCWOSL)	Netherlands
University of Utrecht – KWR Watercycle Research Institute	Netherlands
Water Board De Dommel	Netherlands
Women for Water Partnership and Butterfly Effect	Netherlands
Landcare Research	New Zealand
Norwegian Environment Agency	Norway
Devconsult	Pakistan
Portuguese Water and Waste Services Regulation Authority (ERSAR)	Portugal
Portuguese Water Supply and Wastewater Association (APDA)	Portugal
University of Lisbon	Portugal
National Authority for Public Services (ANRSC)	Romania
Water Industry Commission for Scotland (WICS)	Scotland (United Kingdom)
Water Industry Team, Scottish government	Scotland (United Kingdom)
Permanent Delegation of the Slovak Republic to the OECD	Slovak Republic
Slovenian Water Agency	Slovenia
Water Research Commission (WRC)	South Africa
Adecagua	Spain
Association of Water Supply and Sanitation (AEAS)	Spain
Euro-Mediterranean Water Institute (IEA)/Murcia Water Agency	Spain
ICATALIST/University of Leeds	Spain/United Kingdom
Jucar River Basin Authority	Spain
Madrid Institute of Advanced Studies (IMDEA) – Water	Spain
Stockholm International Water Institute (SIWI)	Sweden
Hydropolitics Association	Turkey
Turkish Water Institute (SUEN)	Turkey
Global Water Partnership	Ukraine
ARUP	United Kingdom
Department for Environment Food and Rural Affairs (Defra)	United Kingdom
Open University	United Kingdom
Water Policy International	United Kingdom
Environmental Protection Agency	United States
Global Water Alliance	United States
University of Arizona Water Resources Research Center (UAWRRC)	United States
Resolute Marine	United States
Scientific Information Centre of Interstate Commission for Water Co-ordination in Central Asia (SIC ICWC)	Uzbekistan

Source: Based on the 85 responses to the survey on the use and dissemination of the *OECD Principles on Water Governance* (15-24 January 2018).

Chapter 2.

OECD Water Governance Indicator Framework

This chapter presents a Water Governance Indicator Framework as a tool for dialogue on the performance of water governance systems at a given scale (city, basin, country or other) and needed changes over time. The chapter provides a description of the framework's rationale, process, content and methodology as a result of a three-year consultation within the OECD Water Governance Initiative. The framework is intended to be used as a multi-stakeholder self-assessment tool across governments, public, private and non-profit sectors rather than as a monitoring or benchmarking tool. An earlier version of the indicator framework was pilot-tested by 12 institutions across the globe between May and November 2017. It is expected that lessons from the application of this indicator framework in the coming years will help fine-tune it if and where needed.

Rationale for assessing water governance

Good water governance seeks to enhance water security, while responding to environmental, economic and social objectives. By considering that "one cannot improve what cannot be assessed", evaluating the governance system in place can help identify gaps and priorities, needs, and responses for effective, efficient and inclusive water policies (Figure 2.1). There is neither a unique way to measure the complexity that the concept of water governance entails, nor a finite number of indicators that can capture the variety of water governance dimensions, along with the diversity of political, historical, legal, administrative, geographic and economic circumstances. However, indicators can raise awareness and address information asymmetries, as a first step towards better water governance.

Figure 2.1. **The water governance policy cycle**

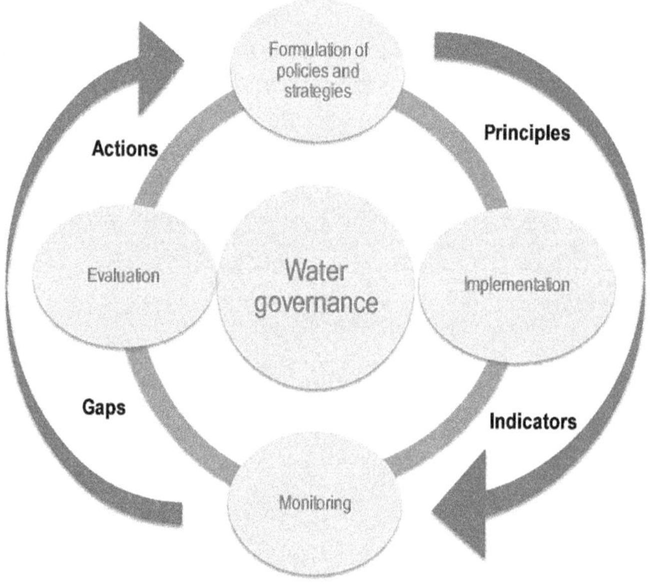

Source: Adapted from OECD (2015a), *OECD Principles on Water Governance*, www.oecd.org/governance/oecd-principles-on-water-governance.htm.

Since the adoption of the *OECD Principles on Water Governance* in 2015, the OECD Water Governance Initiative has developed an implementation strategy based on: 1) an indicator framework to allow a self-assessment of the governance system; and 2) a number of inspirational evolving practices to foster bench learning. The indicator framework does not serve as a monitoring tool to investigate progress against a defined framework. It is also not intended to provide benchmarking across countries, basins, regions and cities, as according to the OECD Principles, governance responses are highly contextual and hardly comparable. Its primary objective is to stimulate a dialogue across stakeholders on what works, what does not, and what should be improved.

While indicators can be helpful in tracking and measuring relevant water governance dimensions, they are not the assessment itself and should be complemented by in-depth evaluations. The proposed indicator framework is considered a contribution to a broader menu of options that can support the implementation of the OECD Principles, which may also include comprehensive analyses (e.g. country-specific policy dialogues) at different levels to provide more in-depth evaluation as well as tailored policy recommendations.

Indicators as a means to an end

Indicators are a means to an end. They support the implementation of the *OECD Principles on Water Governance*, which advocate for place-based policies and consider that water governance systems (more or less formal, complex, and costly) should be designed according to the challenges they are required to address. Indicators can be a vehicle to:

- **Foster dialogue** at local, basin, regional and national levels. They can promote discussion and build consensus across a range of public authorities and stakeholders on the strengths and weaknesses of water governance systems, as well as the ways forward to better manage too much, too little and too polluted water now and in the future.
- **Promote inclusiveness** across stakeholders and identify the role that each can play to contribute to positive spill-overs on water governance. This can be achieved through in-depth consultations across public, private and non-profit institutions on the who can do what to improve water governance as a shared responsibility. As such, getting the evaluation process right is key. It is important to ensure a transparent, non-discriminatory, open and forward-looking process. It is also important to make sure that stakeholders are motivated and that their inputs are taken into consideration.
- **Stimulate transparency** on the performance of water-related institutions. Indicators can reduce information gaps and lead to greater accountability of governments and stakeholders on how they deliver intended outcomes, while shedding light on whether institutional and regulatory arrangements are fit-for-purpose and fit-for-the future.
- **Increase awareness** on specific issues that would otherwise not receive the same attention. They can also enhance data production and collection, as well as promote technical capacity development.
- **Trigger actions to bridge water governance gaps.** In line with the *OECD Principles on Water Governance*, the ultimate goal of the OECD water governance indicators is not just to measure water governance dimensions, but also to collectively identify what works, what does not, and what can be improved. The indicators can inform policy makers and help set policy priorities. Within the context of the global agenda, they can support countries in achieving the Sustainable Development Goal (SDG) 6 on water, as guidance for governments to strengthen institutions' implementation capacity. Implementing SDG 6 requires overcoming a number of gaps that can hinder the achievement of universal access to drinking water and sanitation, reaching a good status of water quality or reducing water stress. For instance, many countries are lagging behind in terms of data production and sharing. Appropriate technical and human capacity is an important challenge for many countries; yet, inadequate funding is a barrier to building and maintaining networks as well as replacing and modernising existing water infrastructures.

Lessons learnt from existing indicators

Two main drivers plead for the development of the OECD Water Governance Indicator Framework. One is to help fill a gap in the literature, since there is no systemic and comprehensive assessment framework of the water governance cycle (from assigning roles and responsibilities to monitoring and evaluation of water policies). The second is to support interested cities, basins, regions and countries with the implementation of the *OECD Principles on Water Governance*.

There has been an increasing trend in the development of water governance indicators, showing both the need for assessment and the challenges in synthesising complex concepts through indicators. In an effort to take stock of existing initiatives, the "OECD inventory: Water governance indicators and measurement frameworks", launched on line in October 2015, mapped 78 instruments (e.g. indicators, maps, databases and assessment tools; see Table 2.2) for measuring and evaluating several water governance aspects. Most of these indicators relate to specific functions (water, sanitation and hygiene and integrated water resources management), scales (e.g. national, basin) or governance dimensions (transparency, capacity, etc.), and rely on experts' views and judgements.

A parallel exercise to take stock of OECD implementation tools also provided useful background on international comparison of public sector performance, including on public procurement, open and inclusive government, accessibility and quality of public services, multi-level governance, public investment and finance. The most relevant toolkits and indicators for the implementation of the *OECD Principles on Water Governance* are summarised in Table 2.1.

Developing water governance indicators

Five main challenges

Five main key challenges can be highlighted when dealing with governance indicators. The challenges are related to the complexity of the water governance dimensions to be assessed; data availability; data collection through expert views; comparability over space and time; and the difficulty in drawing causality linkages between outcomes measured by indicators and policies aiming at generating certain impacts (Figure 2.2).

Figure 2.2. **Five main challenges for developing indicators**

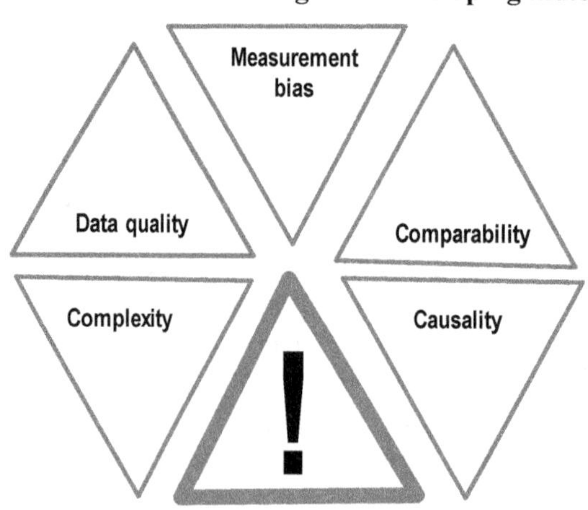

Table 2.1. **Selected supporting tools to OECD legal instruments**

	Link to the *OECD Principles on Water Governance*
Toolkits	
Public Procurement Toolbox (2008 ,updated in 2016) The toolbox is an online knowledge-sharing platform supporting the implementation of the 2015 *OECD Recommendation of the Council on Public Procurement*. It contains evidence-based tools and advice as well as country examples showcasing practices which have been successfully tested in a number of countries. The toolbox was updated in 2016 to mirror the 12 Principles included in the OECD Recommendation: transparency, integrity, access, balance, participation, efficiency, e-procurement, capacity, evaluation, risk management, accountability and integration. They reflect the critical role governance of public procurement must play in achieving and advancing public policy objectives.	– Principle 9 (integrity and transparency)
Effective Public Investment Toolkit (2015) The toolkit was developed to support the implementation of the 2014 *Recommendation of the Council on Effective Public Investment across Levels of Government*. The toolkit includes the rationale for the 12 Principles that compose the Recommendation, examples of concrete actions to take and good practices from countries, as well as indicators and self-assessment questions to monitor the status of each Principle. For each Principle of the Recommendation, suggestions of pitfalls to avoid and potential solutions are also provided.	– Principle 2 (appropriate scales) – Principle 6 (financing) – Principle 3 (policy coherence) – Principle 4 (capacity) – Principle 5 (data and information) – Principle 7 (regulatory framework) – Principle 10 (stakeholder engagement) – Principle 12 (monitoring and evaluation)
High-level Checklist on Financial Regulation (2009) Although not referred to as a toolkit, the checklist was developed as an annex to the *Recommendation of the Council on a Policy Framework for Effective and Efficient Financial Regulation* to guide its practical implementation. For each component of the Recommendation, the checklist suggests key self-assessment questions for countries to evaluate their own state-of-play and areas for improvement in order to prioritise their implementation efforts.	– Principle 6 (financing) – Principle 1 (roles and responsibilities) – Principle 3 (policy coherence) – Principle 9 (integrity and transparency) – Principle 12 (monitoring and evaluation)
Indicator systems	
Public Procurement Key Performance Indicators (2016) The key performance indicators have been developed to support the implementation of several principles towards the performance of public procurement systems: 1) efficiency of the public procurement cycle; 2) openness and transparency of the public procurement; 3) professionalism of the public procurement workforce; 4) contract performance management. The methodology for key performance indicators is currently under revision in line with the *OECD Recommendation of the Council on Public Procurement* (2015).	– Principle 9 (integrity and transparency)
Indicators of Regulatory Policy and Governance (2015) The indicators present up-to-date evidence of OECD member countries' regulatory policy and governance practices advocated in the 2012 *Recommendation of the Council on Regulatory Policy and Governance*. They cover in detail three principles on stakeholder engagement, regulatory impact assessment and *ex post* evaluation, and provide a baseline measurement to track countries' progress over time and identify areas for reform. The indicators are expected to be updated every three to four years.	– Principle 7 (regulatory framework)
Indicators on the co-ordination of public investment across levels of government (2015) The indicators measure the co-ordination mechanisms in place for effective public investment in light of the 2014 *Recommendation of the Council on Effective Public Investment across Levels of Government*. Together, the 12 indicators compose a "co-ordination index" and rely on a dataset covering most OECD countries. Indicators focus on Pillars 1 (co-ordinated planning, strategies across levels of government, jurisdictions, sectors) and 3 (fiscal and regulatory co-ordination) of the Recommendation.	– Principle 2 (appropriate scales) – Principle 6 (financing) – Principle 3 (policy coherence) – Principle 4 (capacity) – Principle 5 (data and information) – Principle 7 (regulatory framework) – Principle 10 (stakeholder engagement) – Principle 12 (monitoring and evaluation)

Table 2.2. **A mapping of water governance indicators and assessment frameworks**

Indicators with water governance components	– The degree of integrated water resources management implementation (Target 6.5), United Nations Development Programme – The amount of water- and sanitation-related official development assistance that is part of a government co-ordinated spending plan (Target 6.a), World Health Organization, United Nations Environment Programme, OECD – The proportion of local administrative units with established and operational policies and procedures for participation of local communities in water and sanitation management (Target 6.b), World Health Organization, United Nations Environment Programme, OECD – Urban Water and Sanitation Governance Index, UN-HABITAT – Groundwater Governance Indicators, Food and Agriculture Organization, UNESCO, Global Environment Facility, World Bank, International Association of Hydrogeologists – Composite index for regulatory governance in the water and wastewater sector, Instituto Superior Técnico – University of Lisbon, Portuguese Water Partnership – Water Management Transparency Index, Transparency International – Equity index in water and sanitation, Luh. et al. – Sustainable Water Governance Index, Iribarnegaray and Seghezzo – Asia Water Governance Index, Araral and Yu – Canadian Water Sustainability Index, Policy Research Initiative – Key performance indicators of river basin organisations, Hooper – Performance indicators of river basin organisations, Network of Asian River Basin Organizations – Performance indicators for African basin organizations, International Network of Basin Organisations – Benchmarking water services, European Benchmarking Co-operation – Performance indicators, ONEMA – Annual Report on Water and Waste Services in Portugal and quality of service indicators assessment system, Portuguese Water and Waste Services Regulation Authority – Comparative analyses of public services for drinking water and sanitation, Fédération nationale des collectivités concédantes et régies (National Federation of Local Water Authorities) – Performance indicators projects, International Water Association – WASH Sustainability Index Tool, USAID-Rotary International – Turin Index, Fondazione Ambiente – Water Security Index, Asian Development Bank – Index to assess the sustainability of water and sanitation management systems, Iribarnegaray et al. – Index of drinking water adequacy (IDWA), Lee Kuan Yew School of Public Policy – Integrated water resources management implementation indicators in South Africa, Water Research Commission – Monitoring progress in the water sector: A selected set of indicators, UN-Water – Groundwater Resources Sustainability Indicators, UNESCO – Environmental Performance Index, Yale University – Country Policy and Institutional Assessment, World Bank – Watershed Sustainability Index, Chaves and Alipaz – Water and Wetland Index, WWF
Databases	– Data Portal, UNEP-DHI IWRM – Water Lex, Food and Agriculture Organization – *Database on Instruments Used for Environmental Policy*, OECD – *Legal Database*, WaterLex – National open data, various countries – *AQUASTAT*, Food and Agriculture Organization – Private Participation in Infrastructure Project Database, World Bank – Global Groundwater Information System (GGIS), International Groundwater Resources Assessment Centre – IBNET, World Bank
Guidelines	– Integrated Water Resources Management Guidelines at River Basin Level, UNESCO-IHP – Water Governance Facility, Stockholm International Water Institute, Water Integrity Network – User' s Guide on Assessing Water Governance, United Nations Development Programme – Freshwater Conservation and Water, Sanitation, and Hygiene Integration Guidelines: A Framework for Implementation in Sub-Saharan Africa, Africa Biodiversity Collaborative Group, Conservation International, and The Nature Conservancy – Multi-level Water Governance Framework, OECD – Guidelines for Drinking-Water Quality (4th ed.), World Health Organization – Promoting transparency, integrity and accountability in the water and sanitation sector in Uganda, Water Integrity Network, Water and Sanitation Program – Global Corruption Report: Climate Change, Transparency International – Cap-Net, Integrated Water Resources Management for River Basin Organizations: Training Manual, United Nations Development Programme

Table 2.2. **A mapping of water governance indicators and assessment frameworks** (*continued*)

Maps	– Environmental Democracy Index, World Resources Institute – Wastewater Treatment Performance Map, Yale University – Water Risk Filter, WWF – Aqueduct Water Risk Framework, World Resources Institute
Assessment tools	– Water and wastewater services in the Danube region: A state of the sector, World Bank, International Association of Water Supply Companies in the Danube River Catchment Area – Benefit of Governance in Drought Adaptation – Governance Assessment Guide, Bressers et al. – Toolkit on Sex-Disaggregated Water Data, United Nations World Water Assessment Programme – Basin report cards, WWF – Global water solidarity, Certificate for Decentralized Water Solidarity, United Nations Development Programme – Freshwater conservation and WASH: Monitoring and evaluation framework and indicators, Africa Biodiversity Collaborative Group, United States Agency for International Development – Best practices in regulating state-owned and municipal water utilities, UN- Economic Commission for Latin America and the Caribbean – The Transboundary Water Assessment Programme, United Nations Environment Programme – AquaRating, Inter-American Development Bank, International Water Association – Ten building blocks for sustainable water governance, van Rijswick et al. – Assessing stability and dynamics in flood risk governance, Dries et al. – The AWS International Water Stewardship Standard, Alliance for Water Stewardship – Country briefs project, UN-Water – Analysis of the Auditor General's Annual Report 2011/12 Uganda, Office of the Auditor General – The UN-Water status report on the application of integrated approaches to WRM, UN-Water – European Water Stewardship Standards, European Water Parternship – Regional water governance benchmarking project, Svendsen et al. – Global analysis and assessment of sanitation and drinking-water, UN-Water, World Health Organization – The Pacific IWRM Project, Global Environment Facility – Status of implementation of CSD-13 policy actions on water and sanitation, United Nations Department of Economic and Social Affairs – Survey of progress towards IWRM, Japan Water Forum – The institutional economics of water, Saleth and Dinar – World Water Development Report. Water: A Shared Responsibility, UN-Water – Protocol on water and health, United Nations Economic Commission for Europe – Access Initiative, World Resources Institute

Source: OECD (2015b), "OECD inventory: Water governance indicators and measurement frameworks", https://www.oecd.org/cfe/regional-policy/Inventory_Indicators.pdf.

Complexity: Measuring governance is not an easy task. Governance is a complex concept, its understanding is open to several interpretations, its measurement is not straightforward, and comparisons across countries or over time are not always possible. The definition of water governance encompasses multiple dimensions (institutional, political, social, environmental and economic ones) and involves a multitude of actors at different levels of government, in the public and in the private sector.

Data quality and availability: "Poor governance produces poor data" and vice versa. On the one hand, the lack of data may hinder the identification of gaps and the measurement of progress year after year; therefore, generating data might favour good governance, as indicators can spot problems, create incentives for changes and trigger changes. On the other hand, to be able to inform decision makers, indicators should be built on a clear set of established objectives rather than on the availability of data, avoiding the risk of obtaining *data-rich* but *information-poor* indicators.

Perception bias: There is no guarantee that perception-based assessments by experts or stakeholders will yield unbiased results. Results will depend on how experts are selected, their knowledge and their experience, as well as their independence from political influence. A wide number of stakeholders with interests at stake in the assessed issues and a certain level of representativeness of different categories of stakeholders can make the process more interactive and open. Nevertheless, rules and methodologies for gathering stakeholder's views should be clearly set ahead. Results based on subjective views can challenge comparisons across times, as it is likely that different experts/stakeholders would provide different answers.

Comparability: Indicators can be set up to monitor and evaluate water governance in specific contexts and for specific scales. Hence, they might not be universally applicable and some adaptations may be needed. Comparability is a concern also in terms of time: over time, data may not be available or the original measurement may no longer be relevant to guide decisions, for instance because of changes in the institutional setting.

Causality: Indicators can inform outcomes of water policies; however, it is difficult to identify the causal linkages between policies and results. In fact, there are a number of factors that can affect results beyond the policy itself, such as fiscal crisis and climate conditions.

A pragmatic approach

Developing governance indicators according to recognised criteria can help overcome the above-mentioned caveats. A number of criteria to assess indicators' quality and adequacy are commonly used to provide guidelines for their selection, such as: Specific, Measurable, Achievable, Relevant and Time-bound (SMART); Relevant, Accepted, Credible, Easy, Robust (RACER); and Clear, Relevant, Economic, Adequate and Monitorable (CREAM) (European Commission, 2017). Inspired by these criteria and by the discussions within the OECD Water Governance Initiative, some key characteristics for water governance indicators have been identified, such as: be relevant (according to the purpose of the measurement); be participative (in their development); be practical (in the production and collection considering resources and time constraints), and be realistic (in terms of how they will be used) (Figure 2.3). Guiding questions are reported in Table 2.3.

Figure 2.3. **Expected characteristics of indicators**

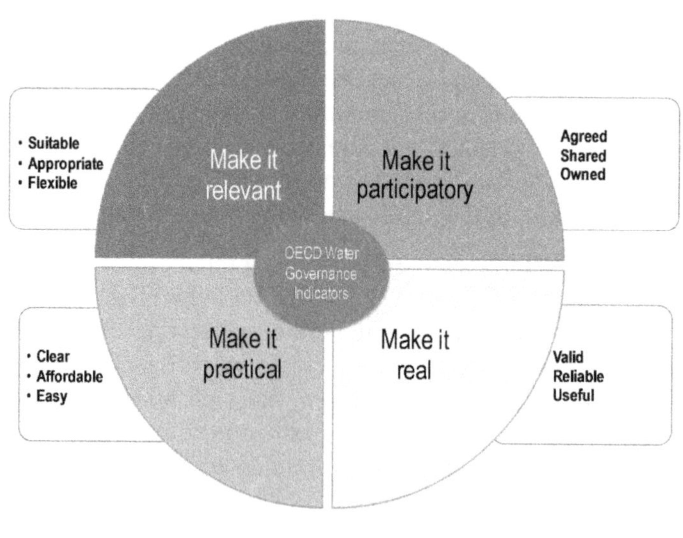

Source: OECD (2015c), "OECD water governance indictors, OECD scoping note".

- **Make it relevant:** Indicators should be suitable for the purpose. In practice, they are meant to clearly respond to the objectives to which they are linked. They should neither be "too specific", incurring the risk of missing information, neither "too broad", failing to capture relevant aspects that can be useful for learning and triggering changes. When developing indicators, it is important to take into account the scale at which they will be applied, their consistency over time and the local circumstances, including geographical and political ones that can affect the results. Indicators can be used to evaluate the performance of specific functions at specific scales (e.g. monitoring performance of utilities, efficiency of institutions in managing water resources at basin level, etc.). However, they can also be broader in scope. In this case, as different bodies are in charge of designing and implementing water policy at various levels, as well as of producing and collecting data, co-ordination across them is a priority concern also in terms of data collection from multiple sources.
- **Make it participatory:** The participation of a broad set of stakeholders in developing a consensus around building indicators is crucial to minimise the risk of "too safe" indicators or "too poorly" measurable ones. Those responsible for implementing the activities might be tempted to construct "easy to get" indicators (mainly data-driven) and "easy-to-meet" targets. On the other hand, when indicators are built by those who are not in charge of monitoring them, they might be too ambitious and less realistic. Developing indicators through a collaborative effort among experts, policy makers and other stakeholders would definitely help reach a balance between these two situations, while drawing from a range of expertise and knowledge. It has been widely acknowledged that communication between the scientists who develop indicators and policy makers is an important step towards streamlining a robust set of indicators. Input-based and bottom-up processes are key to build ownership and ensure collective action, where appropriate, in the production, collection, use and dissemination of data to guide public action.
- **Make it practical:** Once defined, indicators should not lead to extra-administrative burdens (e.g. overlaps of information, heavy bureaucratic procedures, etc.) for data collection and should preferably be accompanied by a system of implicit incentives. For example, reputation effects (results publicly available) and bench learning can encourage efforts towards data collection. Data production and collection should be feasible at the least cost. In the water sector, quantitative and qualitative data on governance are available, but they are often scattered across agencies and institutions. Hence, the challenge is not necessarily to define new indicators, but to adapt those that already exist, co-ordinating across agencies and minimising the administrative costs of producing data.
- **Make it real:** A reality check is necessary to test whether indicators are relevant and useful in measuring water governance aspects or if they redundant, incomplete and inconsistent. Pilot tests help to adjust indicators where needed. A "reality check" helps to understand if indicators are replicable over time, if data are available and if they are able to inform decision makers over time.

Table 2.3. **A checklist for robust indicators**

Objective	Criteria	Questions
Make it relevant	Suitable	Is the indicator fit for the purpose?
	Appropriate	Is the indicator appropriate according to the scale?
	Flexible	Is the indicator adaptable to different scales, time, local circumstances?
Make it participatory	Agreed	Do stakeholders agree on exactly what the indicator measures?
	Shared	Have different views been shared to produce valuable information?
	Owned	Do stakeholders contribute to data production and collection?
Make it practical	Clear	Is the indicator clearly understandable?
	Affordable	Is information available at reasonable cost?
	Easy	Will data be easy to collect?
Make it real	Valid	Has the indicator been validated through a "test "process?
	Reliable	Will the indicator represent a consistent measure over time?
	Useful	Will the information be useful for decision making, accountability and learning?

Source: Criteria and questions have been adapted from: Adaptation Fund (2011), "Project level results framework and baseline guideline document", www.oecd.org/env/cc/48332155.pdf.

The OECD Water Governance Indicator Framework

The Water Governance Indicator Framework is composed of 36 water governance indicators (input and process), and a checklist containing 106questions on water governance. It is complemented by an Action Plan for discussion on future improvements. The Water Governance Indicator Framework is conceived as a self-assessment tool to collectively identify whether framework conditions are in place for each OECD Principle and if they are implemented and properly functioning based on a multi-stakeholder dialogue. The Water Governance Indicator Framework is intended to be applicable at different scales (city, basin, national or other) and for different water management functions (water resources, water services, water disasters) (Figure 2.4).

Figure 2.4. **The OECD Water Governance Indicator Framework**

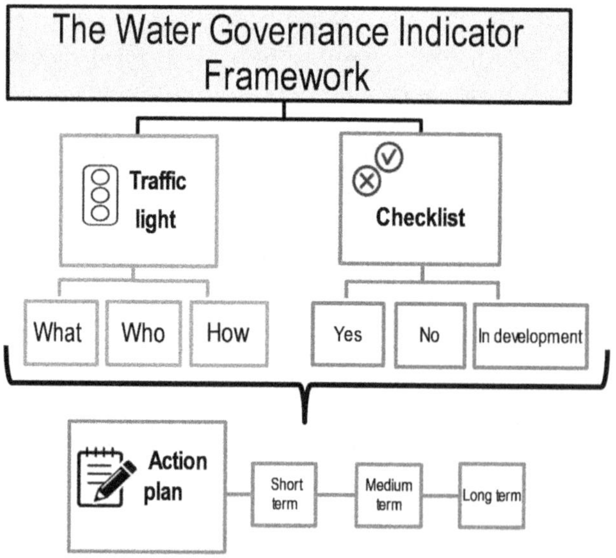

Process

The OECD Water Governance Indicator Framework is the result of a bottom-up process within the OECD Water Governance Initiative (WGI), a platform of 130+ members from the public, private and not-for-profit sectors, gathering twice a year since 2013 to share knowledge, experience and best practices on water governance (Figure 2.5).

Figure 2.5. **The main steps in developing the indicator framework**

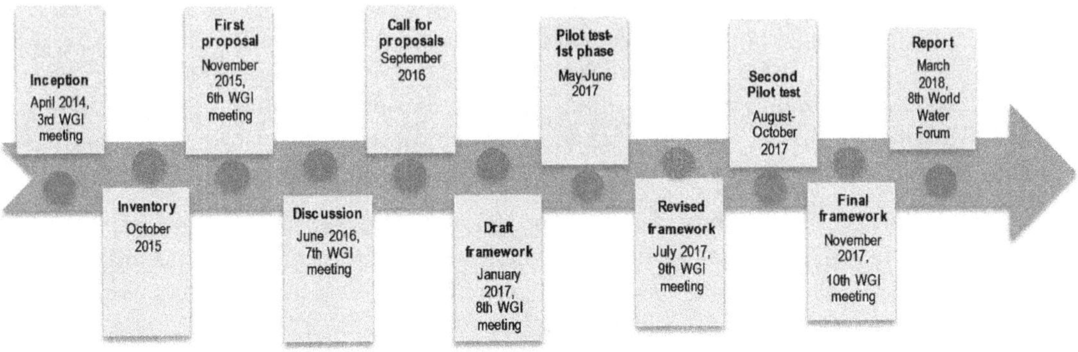

The development process consisted of six main steps: 1) scoping needs; 2) consulting stakeholders; 3) collecting inputs; 4) streamlining; 5) pilot testing; 6) final results.

Scoping needs: The indicators were proposed and discussed within the OECD Water Governance Initiative. Ten key questions guided the discussion (Table 2.4). They clarified the scope, scale, content, process, replicability, uses, producers, beneficiaries, monitoring and disclosure of water governance indicators. It was decided to measure framework conditions and expected changes through input and process indicators; to use experts'/stakeholders' views backed by factual data; to promote a participative approach for data collection through multi-stakeholder workshops; and to use the indicator framework as a self-assessment tool to improve the water policy cycle.

Table 2.4. **Ten key questions for water governance indicators**

Questions	Proposals
What to measure?	Framework conditions and expected changes
Which **type** of indicators?	Input and process indicators
Whose **views**?	Experts'/stakeholders' views and factual data
At which **scale**?	Reflecting the multi-scale dynamics of water governance
Through which **process**?	Multi-stakeholder workshops
Who are the **beneficiaries**?	Governments, river basin organisations, service providers, donor agencies, non-governmental organisations, civil society, emerging actors
Who will **collect** and **produce** data?	Voluntary approach in interested cities, basins, regions and countries
How will the indicators be **used**?	As a self-assessment tool to improve the water policy cycle
How to ensure **replicability**?	Pilot tests at different levels and in different contexts, to provide "reality checks" on data applicability, availability and replicability
How to **disclose the results**?	OECD report and online material

Source: OECD (2015c), "OECD water governance indictors, OECD scoping note".

Consulting stakeholders: Consultations were carried out during the biannual meetings since 2014 (from the fourth to the tenth meeting of the WGI). Multiple interactions occurred within the WGI Working Group on Indicators co-ordinated by the

OECD, the French Scientific and Technical Association for Water and the Environment (ASTEE), Transparency International and International Network of Basin Organisations/Office International de l'Eau (INBO/OIEAU), as well as through dedicated webinars. In addition, intermediate milestones were discussed with the broader water community at global events such as the 7th World Water Forum (Korea, April 2015) and the 26th World Water Week (Stockholm, August 2016).

Collecting inputs: The framework benefited from written inputs from WGI members in the form of 70+ proposed water governance indicators following a call for proposal. A template shared among the members aimed to harmonise the collection of information, in particular: objectives; Principles to which the indicator(s) referred to; water functions and scale; distinction by input, process, output, outcome and impact indicators; beneficiaries and links with the SDGs. Notably, a number of indicators resulted to be cross-cutting across water functions and referring to several Principles, rather than to only one specifically.

Streamlining: The first proposal contained more than 320 proxies to appraise water governance dimensions for each Principle, which were later transformed into indicators. Iterative discussions within the OECD WGI helped streamline the framework into 36 input and process indicators (qualitative indicators) herein presented as part of the traffic light component of the indicator framework. Such indicators were complemented by a checklist of 106 questions, allowing for an in-depth discussion among stakeholders involved in the self-assessment.

Pilot testing: Two rounds of tests were carried out by 12 pilots to check the relevance of the proposed framework and to collect data. Twelve pilot countries, OECD countries and non-OECD economies, provided a reality check on the robustness and coherence of the indicators; their relevance to appraise the effectiveness, efficiency and inclusiveness of water governance systems; and the feasibility of data collection (Box 2.1). Compared to the first phase of the pilot test, the second phase helped stakeholders to focus in depth on each dimension of the indicators and initiate a debate likely to continue in the future.

Box 2.1. The pilot tests of the OECD Water Governance Indicator Framework

Pilot testers' characteristics

Pilot testers facilitated the stakeholder consultation and took the lead in drafting the synthesis report as well as in collecting data. In March 2017, the OECD Secretariat issued a call for pilot testing the Water Governance Indicator Framework. Any government authority or public, private or non-profit stakeholder involved in local, basin, regional or national level water management operating in any of the water-related sub-sectors (water services, water resources, water disasters) and/or scale of governance (local, regional, basin, national or global) was allowed to apply. The endorsement of the *OECD Principles on Water Governance* (and being familiar with their content) was a prerequisite to carry out the pilot test in a relatively short period of time. Representatives from OECD countries and non-OECD economies alike were eligible to apply. They were requested to meet the following additional prerequisites: proven experience or capacity to convene key stakeholders to discuss and share views on water governance issues at city, region, basin or national levels; proven knowledge or practical experience with indicators or measurement frameworks to assess the performance; track record of pilot testing evaluation processes, mechanisms or frameworks and drawing lessons in terms of how to do it and with whom; proven role in a multi-stakeholder platform discussing water management in a given city, region, basin or country (e.g. member, convener, facilitator, etc.); available resources to organise the multi-stakeholder workshop (be it physical or virtual) in co-operation with the OECD Secretariat and working group co-ordinators; analytical capacity to draft the resulting report compiling the outcomes of the consultation, and convening power to collect the data from stakeholders once the indicator was finalised. A total of 12 applications were received, all of which were eligible to carry out the pilot test (Table 2.5).

Box 2.1. **The pilot tests of the OECD Water Governance Indicator Framework** *(continued)*

Table 2.5. **The pilot testers**

Authority/organisation	Scale	Pilot name	Country	Workshop date 1st pilot test	Workshop date 2nd pilot test
Association for Water & Gas	National	Austria	Austria	23 May 2017	12 September and 6 October 2017
National Water Authority	National	Cabo Verde	Cabo Verde	26 May 2017	x
National Water Authority	National	Peru	Peru	30 May 2017	12 October 2017
Scottish government	Regional	Scotland, United Kingdom	Scotland, United Kingdom	25 May 2017	3 October 2017
Deltares	Province	Eindhoven & Helmond	Netherlands	24 May 2017	11 October 2017
International Secretariat for Water	Basin	Rimac	Peru	10 and 17 May 2017	11 October 2017
Jucar Hydrographic Confederation	Basin	Jucar	Spain	1 June 2017	11 October 2017
Sebou River Basin Agency	Basin	Sebou	Morocco	18 May 2017	10 October 2017
Selangor Water Authority	Basin	Selangor	Malaysia	25 May 2017	11 October 2017
Spanish Association of Water Supply and Sanitation (AEAS)	Basin	Segura	Spain	7 June 2017	3 November 2017
World Wide Fund (WWF) Colombia	Basin	Rio Nare in Antioquia	Colombia	30 May 2017	23 October 2017
Global Water Partnership	Local	Kinshasa	Democratic Republic of Congo	26 September 2017 (one single session for the whole exercise)	

Note: Cabo Verde could not organise the second workshop due to the need to concentrate all available human and financial resources to the water emergency currently in place.

Source: OECD (2017a), "Draft OECD water governance indicators".

Phase I

The objective of the first pilot test was to provide a reality check to help collect evidence and concrete feedback on how the proposed indicator framework was fit to support self-assessment of water governance in a given city, region, basin or country through a multi-stakeholder dialogue. In practice, the selected pilot testers were requested to organise a half-day multi-stakeholder consultation/workshop to gather the key players of water governance at the scale considered for the pilot test. The lead institutions of the 12 pilot tests agreed that the traffic light system was a useful methodology to reflect the existence and the level of implementation of water governance dimensions. The tool was considered easy to understand, helpful in prioritising actions and organising stakeholders' inputs. A total of 80% of pilot testers agreed on the five options of the traffic light system for assessing policy frameworks, institutions and instruments. While a total of 73% of pilot testers considered that the indicators proposed in the traffic light system were relevant to all scales (e.g. national, basin, regional and local), some pilot testers pointed out that the framework seemed to be more valid at a national level. A total of 90% of the pilot testers claimed that the indicators were relevant to all water management functions (e.g. water services, water resources and water disasters). A total of 70% of pilot testers agreed that the traffic light should not only provide a static picture of the current performance, but also an indication of the expected trends over the coming three years. An alternative proposal would consist in evaluating changes every five years (short term) and/or ten years (long term). A challenge consisted in finding a balance between how prescriptive the framework should have been and how open for interpretation. A total of 50% of pilot testers agreed on the need for more guidance on the colour categorisation as well as on the use and implementation of the indicator framework. Others claimed that free interpretation of some aspects of the indicator framework could provide more flexibility to the dialogue but also less comparability. Finally, some pilot testers highlighted that some dimensions were open to several interpretations. These issues helped revise the indicator framework for submission to the second phase of the pilot test.

Box 2.1. **The pilot tests of the OECD Water Governance Indicator Framework** *(continued)*

Phase II

The objective of the second phase of the pilot test was to collect data, while sharing information and knowledge among stakeholders. In most of the cases, the discussion on data underlying the indicators and the consensus among stakeholders on the level of implementation of water governance dimensions was carried out through roundtables and open discussions during the workshops, chaired by the lead institution. In some cases, the discussion consisted of providing feedback on the pre-filled indicator framework by the lead institution. In case of need of further information, or due to time constraints during the workshop, written comments were also provided by the stakeholders involved in the process after the workshop. In some cases, stakeholders were asked to provide inputs in advance for each of the 36 indicators regarding the existence of the water governance dimension and their level of implementation. Then, results of the scoring were discussed in a plenary setting, in addition to their views on the expected changes for the future. This helped to identify the level of consensus amongst stakeholders. To deal with the variety of points of views, due to different backgrounds, experiences or interests, some pilot testers proceeded by raised hands votes for both the traffic light and the checklist. When a high degree of consensus took place, those dissenting were asked to provide reasons or arguments on why they did not agree with the majority. Finally, one pilot tester organised workshops both at the national and regional levels to better capture local differences and needs. Overall, the exercise stimulated dialogue among stakeholders and information sharing, but it also highlighted some challenges. Because pilot tests were used by lead institutions either to assess the water governance system in place or to provide feedback on how to improve the indicator framework, results are quite diverse from one pilot to another in terms of content (data collected) and process (how to organise the self-assessment).

There were major challenges in organising and carrying out the workshops related to the difficulty in gathering stakeholders and to the limited time available for the discussion. Some pilot testers reported the need for further financial resources, for instance to support the participation in the workshops of non-governmental organisations (e.g. travel costs). Pilot testers also conveyed that further tests would be needed to check the applicability of the indicator framework at the local scale. As per data collection, pilot testers found it challenging to respond to some proposed quantitative indicators, which were meant to provide a synthetic picture of key characteristics concerning water management and governance at a certain scale. To the extent possible, the requested "key data" tried to rely on available data from official national statistics as well as parallel reporting from global processes such as the targets of SDG 6 within the 2030 Development Agenda, or the Water Framework Directives for EU countries and others subject to it. These quantitative indicators initially related to both water governance (e.g. institutions, financing, transparency and integrity)[1] and management (e.g. water quality, quantity, water stress).[2] Collecting these data proved to be challenging not only because of the lack of time, but also because of limited data availability at specific scales and the need for further co-ordination across agencies/organisations. Even though quantitative indicators were not meant to serve for benchmarking purposes, further clarifications, descriptions and possibly an indication of the assessment methods would be needed in the future to avoid several interpretations and make sure that they actually play their intended roles.

Notes: 1. Examples are: number of service providers supplying drinking water and sanitation; investment needs projected for the next 10-20 years in water-related infrastructure; number of investigations/prosecutions/sanctions for violations of integrity in procurement in the water sector. 2. Examples are: proportion of population using safely managed drinking water services (SDG 6.1, Indicator 6.1.1); proportion of population using safely managed sanitation services, including a hand-washing facility with soap and water (SDG 6.2, Indicator 6.1.2); share of water abstracted by type of origin (underground, surface).

Source: OECD (2017a), "Draft OECD water governance indicators"; OECD (2017b), "OECD water governance indicators".

Results: Results from Phase I of the pilot test highlighted that the indicator framework was a useful exercise to self-assess the water governance system and it also helped to find ways forward for improvements by stimulating dialogue. For this purpose, the self-assessment tool was complemented by an "Action Plan" in Phase II to report on actions already in place or planned to improve those aspects of the water governance system which at the time of the investigation did not reach a satisfactory level of implementation. Suggestions by pilot testers helped to improve the indicator framework and refine the language. Results from Phase II, which are available on line,[1] helped develop guidance for end users to carry out the self-assessment, engage stakeholders and collect data.

Objectives

The Water Governance Indicator Framework aims to appraise water governance systems over the short, medium and long term (Figure 2.6):

- Short term: existence and level of implementation of the framework conditions of the water governance system in place. This assessment provides a static view of who does what and how.
- Medium term: expected changes over time in the water governance system. Compared to the "static" assessment of identifying the existence of framework conditions, this phase of the assessment aims to be a "dynamic" one. It gathers stakeholders' views on expected changes over time in order to improve the water governance systems. Repeating the assessment every three years would allow comparing progress against the baseline (static assessment) and verifying whether expectations match the reality (dynamic assessment).
- Long term: impacts of water governance arrangements. This measurement could ultimately help determine if governance played a role in achieving the desired water management and socio-economic outcomes despite the difficulty to establish causal linkages between policies and results.

Traffic light

The traffic light system contains 36 indicators, 3 for each of the 12 Principles (Table 2.6). They aim to identify the following dimensions:

- The "what" captures the policy and legal frameworks that represent the basis for the allocation of roles and responsibilities, the development of water policies and the implementation of water governance instruments.
- The "who" identifies formal institutions in charge of defining, implementing and evaluating water policies, as well as developing projects and programmes and producing and collecting data, etc.
- The "how" reports on the instruments through which water policies are implemented and evaluated.

Indicators proposed in the traffic light system are a combination of input and process ones (Box 2.2). Through input indicators it is possible to account for the existence of legislation and policy instruments; the process indicators account for actions contributing to the achievement of outcomes (e.g. co-ordination and monitoring instruments). Indicators combine *de jure* (rules-based) indicators, since they concern legal, policy, and regulatory inputs and processes and *de facto* ones since they seek to capture the level of implementation of existing water governance dimensions (UNDP et al., 2013).

Figure 2.6. **The evaluation framework and timeline**

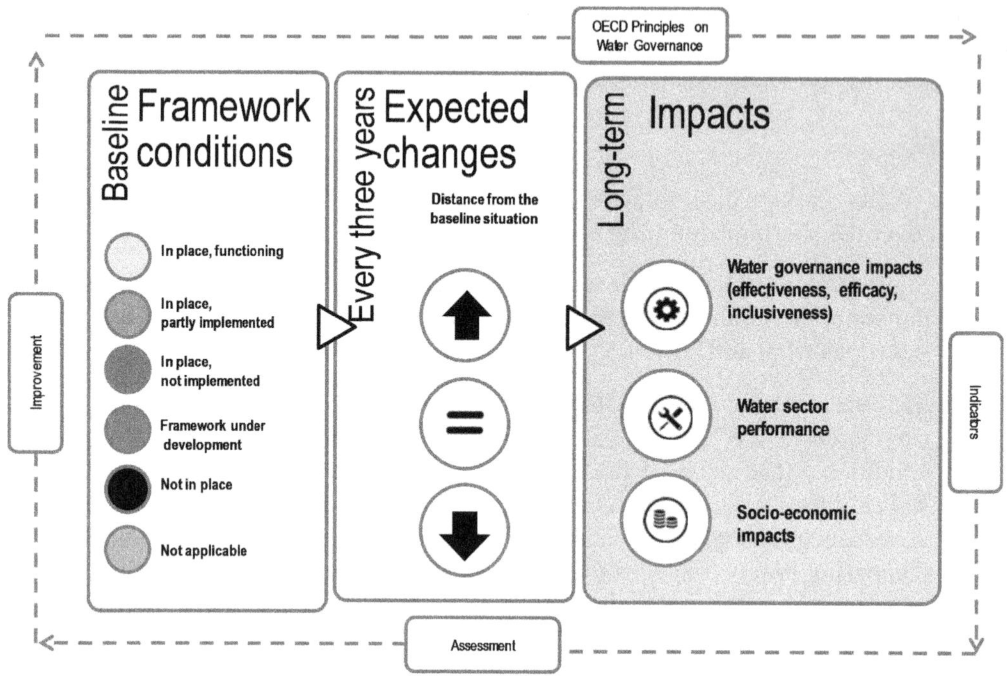

Notes: The current OECD Water Governance Indicator Framework does not provide impact indicators in this first instance. It is based on the lessons learnt from the use of the indicator framework in the years to come, impact indicators could be developed in the future. To ensure broader dissemination and take account of colour printing constraints, the traffic light is herein composed of a scale of blue and grey shades. However, the online indicator brochure and pilot test results reflect the typical traffic light colours.

Source: OECD (2015c), "OECD water governance indicators: OECD scoping note".

Box 2.2. **Typology of indicators**

Depending on what they measure and when, indicators can be distinguished as input, process, output, outcome or impact indicators. Input indicators can measure the inputs needed to produce the outputs, e.g. in terms of legal and policy instruments, human/financial resources; process indicators monitor actions contributing to the achievement of outcomes (e.g. planning, budgeting, service delivery, etc.); output indicators are related to results of inputs and process, for example in terms of the number of wastewater treatment plants built, the volume of water produced, fees collected, etc.; outcome indicators measure short- to medium-term results generated by such outputs (e.g. service expansion and quality improvement); impact indicators measure usually long-term results (e.g. improved health, water security) (Figure 2.7).

Figure 2.7. **An assessment framework: From input to impact indicators**

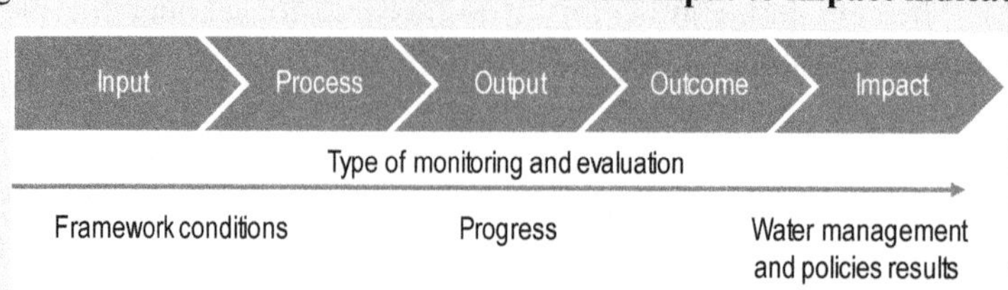

Source: Adapted from UNDP et al. (2013), "User's guide in assessing water governance", www.undp.org/content/undp/en/home/librarypage/democratic-governance/oslo_governance_centre/user-s-guide-on-assessing-water-governance.html.

Methodology for the traffic light system

Data collection is based on objective information and stakeholders'/experts' perceptions: the former documents the existence of policy, legal, and institutional frameworks and tools; the latter captures the level of implementation through subjective judgments. Data are collected by means of a five-scale assessment (plus a "not applicable "option). Respondents are required to choose the colour corresponding to the level of implementation at the moment in which the assessment is carried out (traffic light baseline at *n*). Results are visualised through the use of a wheel containing the colour corresponding to the evaluation (Figure 2.11). The colours correspond to the assessments described below which respond to the question "What is the current situation?" (Figure 2.8).

Table 2.6. **OECD water governance indicators**

Principle	Indicators
Principle 1: Roles and responsibilities	**Indicator 1.a:** Existence and level of implementation of a water law **Indicator 1.b:** Existence and functioning of ministry, line ministry, central agency with core water-related responsibilities for policy making **Indicator 1.c:** Existence and implementation of mechanisms to review roles and responsibilities, to diagnose gaps and adjust when need be
Principle 2: Appropriate scale(s)	**Indicator 2.a:** Existence and level of implementation of integrated water resources management policies and strategies **Indicator 2.b:** Existence and functioning of institutions managing water at the hydrographic scale **Indicator 2.c:** Existence and level of implementation of co-operation mechanisms for the management of water resources across water-related users and levels of government from local to basin, regional, national and upper scales
Principle 3: Policy coherence	**Indicator 3.a:** Existence and level of implementation of cross-sectoral policies and strategies promoting policy coherence between water and key related areas, in particular environment, health, energy, agriculture, land use and spatial planning **Indicator 3.b:** Existence and functioning of an inter-ministerial body or institutions for horizontal co-ordination across water-related policies **Indicator 3.c:** Existence and level of implementation of mechanisms to review barriers to policy coherence and/or areas where water and related practices, policies or regulations are misaligned
Principle 4: Capacity	**Indicator 4.a:** Existence and level of implementation of hiring policies based on a merit-based and transparent professional and recruitment process of water professionals independent from political cycles **Indicator 4.b:** Existence and functioning of mechanisms to identify and address capacity gaps in water institutions **Indicator 4.c:** Existence and level of implementation of educational and training programmes for water professionals
Principle 5: Data and information	**Indicator 5.a:** Existence and functioning of updated, timely shared, consistent and comparable water information systems **Indicator 5.b:** Existence and functioning of public institutions, organisations and agencies in charge of producing, co-ordinating and disclosing standardised, harmonised and official water-related statistics **Indicator 5.c:** Existence and level of implementation of mechanisms to identify and review data gaps, overlaps and unnecessary overload
Principle 6: Finance	**Indicator 6.a:** Existence and level of implementation of governance arrangements that help water institutions collect the necessary revenues to meet their mandates and drive water-sustainable and efficient behaviours **Indicator 6.b:** Existence and functioning of dedicated institutions in charge of collecting water revenues and allocating them at the appropriate scale **Indicator 6.c:** Existence and level of implementation of mechanisms to assess short-, medium- and long-term investment and operational needs and ensure the availability and sustainability of such finance
Principle 7: Regulatory frameworks	**Indicator 7.a:** Existence and level of implementation of a sound water management regulatory framework to foster enforcement and compliance, achieve regulatory objectives in a cost-effective way, and protect the public interest **Indicator 7.b:** Existence and functioning of dedicated public institutions responsible for ensuring key regulatory functions for water services and resources management **Indicator 7.c:** Existence and level of implementation of regulatory tools to foster the quality of regulatory processes for water management at all levels
Principle 8: Innovative water governance practices	**Indicator 8.a:** Existence and level of implementation of policy frameworks and incentives fostering innovation in water management practices and processes **Indicator 8.b:** Existence and functioning of institutions encouraging bottom-up initiatives, dialogue and social learning as well as experimentation in water management at different levels **Indicator 8.c:** Existence and level of implementation of knowledge and experience-sharing mechanisms to bridge the divide between science, policy and practice

Table 2.6. **OECD water governance indicators** (*continued*)

Principle	Indicators
Principle 9: Integrity and transparency	**Indicator 9.a:** Existence and level of implementation of legal and institutional frameworks (not necessarily water-specific) on integrity and transparency which also apply to water management at large **Indicator 9.b:** Existence and functioning of independent courts (not necessarily water-specific) and supreme audit institutions that can investigate water-related infringements and safeguard the public interest **Indicator 9.c:** Existence and level of implementation of mechanisms (not necessarily water-specific) to identify potential drivers of corruption and risks in all water-related institutions at different levels, as well as other water integrity and transparency gaps
Principle 10: Stakeholder engagement	**Indicator 10.a:** Existence and level of implementation of legal frameworks to engage stakeholders in the design and implementation of water-related decisions, policies and projects **Indicator 10.b:** Existence and functioning of organisational structures and responsible authorities to engage stakeholders in water-related policies and decisions **Indicator 10.c:** Existence and level of implementation of mechanisms to diagnose and review stakeholder engagement challenges, processes and outcomes
Principle 11: Trade-offs across water users, rural and urban areas, and generations	**Indicator 11.a:** Existence and level of implementation of formal provisions or legal frameworks fostering equity across water users, rural and urban areas, and generations **Indicator 11.b:** Existence and functioning of an Ombudsman or institution(s) to protect water users, including vulnerable groups **Indicator 11.c:** Existence and level of implementation of mechanisms or platforms to manage trade-offs across users, territories and/or over time in a non-discriminatory, transparent and evidence-based manner
Principle 12: Monitoring and evaluation	**Indicator 12.a:** Existence and level of implementation of policy frameworks promoting regular monitoring and evaluation of water policy and governance **Indicator 12.b:** Existence and functioning of institutions in charge of monitoring and evaluation of water policies and practices and able to help adjust where need be **Indicator 12.c:** Existence and level of implementation of monitoring and evaluation mechanisms to measure to what extent water policy fulfils the intended outcomes and water governance frameworks are fit-for-purpose

Figure 2.8. **What is the current situation of water governance performance?**

Traffic light baseline					
In place, functioning	In place, partly implemented	In place, not implemented	Framework under development	Not in place	Not applicable

Source: OECD (2017c), "Draft OECD water governance indicators".

- In place, functioning: The governance dimension under investigation is complete and relevant in all aspects, no major concerns are noted.
- In place, partly implemented: The governance dimension under investigation is in place, but the level of implementation is not complete. It might be the case that parts are explicitly lacking to make the framework complete. There might be several reasons for this, including insufficient funding, regulatory burdens, bureaucratic lengthy processes, etc.
- In place, not implemented: The governance dimension under investigation is in place, but it is not implemented. For example, it can be inactive or activities are of very low relevance to play a real role in possible progress.
- Framework under development: The governance dimension under investigation does not exist yet but the framework is under development.
- Not in place: The governance dimension under investigation does not exist and there are no plans or actions taken for developing it.
- Not applicable: The governance dimension under investigation is not applicable to the context where the self-assessment takes place.

Respondents were also required to identify the expected trend over the coming three years in terms of improvements, decreases or stable situations, compared to the assessment related to baseline scenario. Decreases from the current situation might be due to a decrease in terms of human and financial resources (Figure 2.9). Results reflecting the three-year expected changes are visualised through spider graphs, through which responses (colours) have been transformed into a scale from 0 to 6 (Figure 2.11).

Figure 2.9. **Are changes expected in three years' time on water governance performance?**

Expected progress (three years after the baseline)		
Improvement: ↗	Stable: =	Decrease: ↘

Source: OECD (2017c), "Draft OECD water governance indicators".

Finally, in order to reflect the diversity of opinions during the discussion, respondents were requested to signal the level of consensus among stakeholders. Visually, the level of consensus is represented by an increasing number of drops, from one to three, respectively reflecting weak, acceptable and strong consensus. This aims to take into account the variety of views shared during the multi-stakeholder workshops and stimulate a discussion (Figure 2.10).

Figure 2.10. **Do all stakeholders agree on the assessment made?**

Results of stakeholder consultation		
Strong consensus:	Acceptable consensus:	Weak consensus:

Source: OECD (2017c), "Draft OECD water governance indicators".

Accompanying checklist

In addition to the water governance indicators, the self-assessment includes a checklist of questions concerning the implementation of the 12 Principles (Table 2.7). These questions were formulated on the basis of desk research and previous OECD work, given the limited number of qualitative indicators linked to each Principle (36). It was recognised that a debate on the implementation of each Principle cannot be limited to three indicators and requires a reflection on a number of additional governance conditions, which feature in the checklist. Respondents can answer the questions through: yes, no, in development or not applicable. In addition, they should be able to provide sources/references in order to cross-check the assessment.

Figure 2.11. **Final visualisation of the traffic light**

What is the current situation?

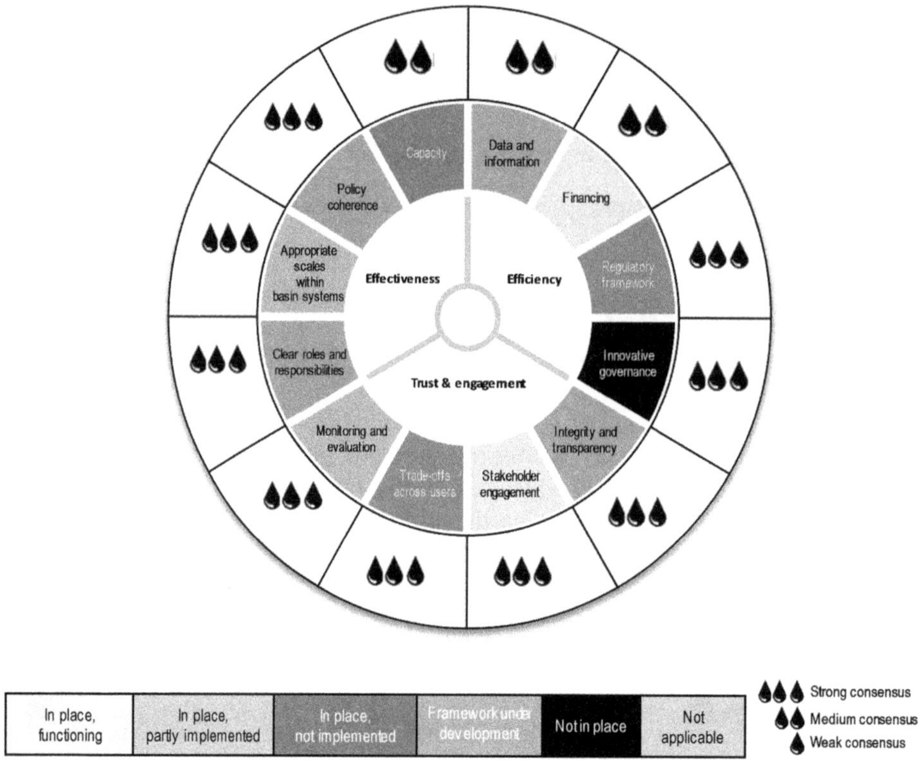

Are changes expected in three years' time?

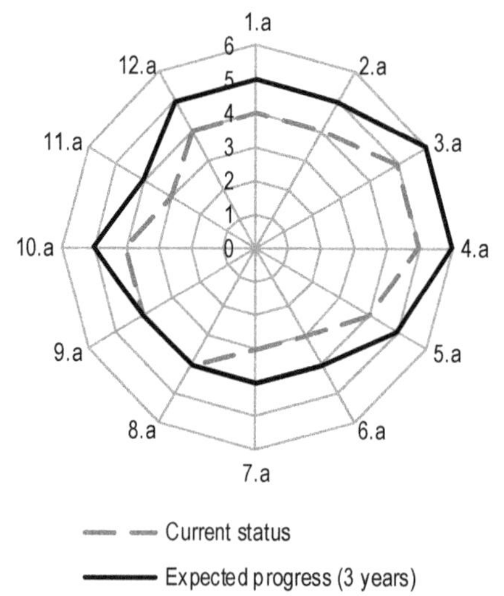

Notes: 0) Not applicable; 1) Not in place; 2) Framework under development; 3) In place, not implemented; 4) In place, partly implemented; 5) In place, functioning; 6) Expected to function better compared to the baseline assessment.

Source: OECD (2017c), "Draft OECD water governance indicators".

Table 2.7. **Checklist for the *OECD Principles on Water Governance***

Principle 1: Roles and responsibilities
Is there a dedicated water policy, indicating goals, duties, resources needed?
Have applicable binding and non-binding water-related international or supranational frameworks and regulations been transposed at national (or subnational) level(s)?
Are there horizontal co-ordination mechanisms across subnational authorities to manage interdependencies for water policy design and implementation?
Are there vertical co-ordination mechanisms or incentives that foster policy alignment, complementarities and co-operation across central and subnational governments?
Principle 2: Appropriate scales within basin systems
Where they exist, do catchment-based organisations have the adequate level of autonomy, staff and budget to carry out their functions?
Are there policy and economic instruments in place to manage too much, too little and too polluted water at hydrographic scale?
In case of transboundary rivers, lakes or aquifers, are there mechanisms or incentives to co-ordinate among riparian states?
Are there co-ordination mechanisms to combine territorial and hydrographic scales for water resources management, for instance in metropolitan areas?
Principle 3: Policy coherence
Is there a dedicated policy or high-level political support to water management as a driver to economic growth as featured by the Sustainable Development Goals?
Are data and projections on water demanded from agriculture, industry (including energy) and households available and guiding decisions about handling competing uses now and in the future?
Is there an assessment of the distributional impacts on water management of decisions taken in other areas?
Are costs due to absent/poor water-related policy coherence evaluated and available to decision makers?
Are benefits from policy coherence and policy complementarities evaluated and showcased to decision makers and key stakeholders?
Are there provisions, frameworks or instruments to ensure that decisions taken in other sectors are water-wise?
Are there horizontal co-ordination mechanisms at subnational and national levels?
Are there conflict mitigation and resolution mechanisms to manage trade-offs across water-related policy areas?
Principle 4: Capacity
Are there incentives to create water careers in the public sector?
Are there guidelines or standards for capacity building across authorities at all levels?
Are there peer-to-peer dialogue platforms across river basin organisations?
Are there networks of utilities and networks of basin organisations at national level?
Are institutional strengthening and soft capacity included in technical assistance programmes?
Are there decentralised co-operation mechanisms to foster north-south, south-south and north-north experience learning, capacity building and knowledge transfer?
Principle 5: Data and information
Are key data on water and sanitation services available?
Are key data on water services publicly available and communicated to customers?
Is the water supply and sanitation information system harmonised, integrated, standardised and co-ordinated across relevant agencies and responsible authorities across relevant governance scales?
Are key data on integrated water resources management (IWRM) available?
Are key data on water resources management publicly available and communicated to users?
Is the IWRM water information system harmonised, integrated, standardised and co-ordinated across relevant agencies and responsible authorities across relevant governance scales?
Are key data on risk management available?

Table 2.7. **Checklist for the *OECD Principles on Water Governance*** (*continued*)

Are key data on water risk management publicly available and communicated to citizens?
Is the risk management water information system harmonised, integrated, standardised and co-ordinated across relevant agencies and responsible authorities across relevant governance scales?
Are there real-time data and do they guide decision making?
Are there bottom-up mechanisms to produce and disclose water-related data and information in a shared responsibility across levels of government, public, private and non-profit stakeholders?
Are there platforms for dialogue between data producers and users?
Are there incentives or forms of co-operation between primary and other data producers?
Do online platforms/tools/agreements exist for experience and knowledge sharing?
Do incentives exist to produce, disclose and use water-related data and information, through innovative ways?
Principle 6: Finance
Are there enough financial revenues (taxes, tariffs, transfers) to cover operational costs and long-term assets renewal, to protect ecosystems services and to finance biodiversity programmes?
Is there a standardised/harmonised guidance at national or subnational level for setting and governing economic instruments such as tariffs, abstraction or pollution charges, groundwater tax?
Are abstraction charges in place to foster water use efficiency and collect revenues?
Are pollution charges in place to foster water quality management and collect revenues?
Are there schemes or incentives for payment for environmental services?
Do flexible and solidarity mechanisms exist in case of water-related disasters?
Are there multi-annual strategic plans to review short-, medium- and long-term investment needs and support policy continuity?
Are there investment plans and programmes and do they guide decision making?
Are there clear budget transparency principles and rules applied at all levels of government?
Are there measures to minimise unnecessary administrative burdens when collecting and disbursing water-related revenues?
Are there reporting mechanisms and audits of financial administration for water-related expenditure?
Are there mechanisms or incentives to foster the efficient and transparent allocation of water-related revenues?
Principle 7: Regulatory frameworks
Is there a systematic requirement to consider existing international standards and norms in the development and revision of national and/or subnational legal frameworks?
Are there dedicated regulatory agency(ies)/bodies or capacities (e.g. within a ministry) in charge of enforcement and compliance for water resources, water services and disaster risk management?
When they exist are regulatory agencies subject to by laws or internal regulations that clearly state their mandate and powers?
Are relevant regulatory and inspection authorities embedded with resources in line with their mandate? In case of dedicated regulatory agency(ies), are they financially independent?
Do regulatory authorities take decisions that can be also legally binding?
Are evaluation mechanisms in place to systematically and regularly performance/effectiveness, gaps and overlaps in the regulatory framework?
Are water-related legislations subject to regulatory impact assessment?
Are there reviews of the governance and performance of regulatory and inspection agencies or bodies?
Are there water specific inspectors (e.g. a water "police") or other specific enforcement tools in place?
Are there co-ordination instruments between water relevant ministries and bodies?
Are there requirements to disclose information and inputs used for regulatory decisions?

Table 2.7. **Checklist for the *OECD Principles on Water Governance*** (*continued*)

Can regulatory decisions taken be repealed?
Are there mechanisms to solve water-related disputes (be they water-specific or not)?
Where self-regulation mechanisms exist, are they object of regular performance assessment?
Principle 8: Innovative governance
Are there any public bodies or accredited bodies fostering innovation (financing, sharing feedback, assessing, incentivising)?
Do innovative tools and processes exist to build capacities, raise awareness, engage stakeholders, share information, and engage within and across organisations?
Are information and communication technologies used to guide better public action in water management and how?
Are there reviews to evaluate the state of play of and potential for technical and non-technical innovation, costs/benefits of innovation, as well as regulations and standards hindering innovation?
Do platforms exist to draw lessons from failures in water policy and governance, and to catalyse and scale-up best practices and success stories?
Are there innovative co-operation mechanisms across territories and water users?
Principle 9: Integrity and transparency
When roles and responsibilities for water supply and sanitation service delivery, water resources management or disaster risk reduction are delegated to dedicated public or private entities, are there contractual arrangements between organising and executive bodies?
Are relevant international conventions, resolutions or frameworks related to transparency and integrity transposed into national legislation?
Are there institutional anticorruption plans, codes of conduct or charters?
Are executive, legislative and judiciary powers clearly separated?
Are there provisions for whistle-blower protection in legal and institutional frameworks? Are whistle-blower policies internalised within all public water sector organisations?
Are corruption risks and actual corruption in the water sector diagnosed?
Are there evaluation tools to track budget transparency in the water sector?
Are water accounts separated to ensure traceability of the water money?
Are there evaluation tools to track reporting on nepotisms and graft; evasion of rules and regulations; political capture; fraud; unethical practices, including those linked with petty corruption manipulated accounting; bad corporate management?
Are there mechanisms/tools to track transparency, accountability and participation in the water sector?
Are there mechanisms to assess the economic, social and environmental costs of water-related corruption?
Are there processes and/or platforms for dialogue on the drivers to corruption and malpractices?
Are there requirements in place for regular financial disclosure of assets, income and interests?
Are anti-bribery management systems in place?
Principle 10: Stakeholder engagement
Are the Arhus Convention and/or other legal and institutional frameworks for stakeholder engagement adopted?
Is a stakeholder mapping carried out to make sure that all those who have a stake in the outcome or that are likely to be affected are clearly identified, and their responsibilities, core motivations and interactions understood?
Are the ultimate line of decision making, the objectives of stakeholder engagement and the expected use of inputs clearly defined?
Are there mechanisms or regular assessment of stakeholder engagement costs or obstacles at large?

Table 2.7. **Checklist for the *OECD Principles on Water Governance*** (*continued*)

Is needed information for result-oriented stakeholder engagement shared?
Is the type and level of engagement customised and the process flexible to adjust to changing circumstances?
Is there a national multi-stakeholder co-ordination platform including representatives from public, private and non-profit sectors and different categories of users?
Are there mechanisms in place to engage science in decision making?
Are there formal and informal mechanisms to engage stakeholders?
Do tailored communication strategies exist for relevant stakeholders, including the general public, regarding all aspects of water management?
Principle 11: Trade-offs across water users, rural and urban areas, and generations
Are there requirements/frameworks for prioritisation among water uses in case of scarcity or emergency situations?
Are there explicit measures in place to identify access to water services by vulnerable groups, such as First Nation communities, refugees, economic migrants and the homeless?
Are rural-urban linkages clearly identified and addressed in water management?
Are there social tariffs or other measures for vulnerable categories of water users?
Are the capacity to pay and willingness to pay of water users evaluated through solid economic analysis and dedicated surveys?
Are analyses for supporting decision making carried out in case of conflicting objectives across users, or geographical/social disparities in accessing water resources and services?
Principle 12: Monitoring and evaluation
Do formal requirements exist for evaluation and monitoring?
Are there agreed-upon key performance indicators?
Do monitoring and reporting mechanisms exist?
Are there provisions or incentives for civil society monitoring?
Are there financial resources available to train civil society organisations in project monitoring?
Are the results of the monitoring and evaluation process shared with the wider public?
Does a national co-ordination platform or alike produce reports for parliamentarian discussion on water issues?

The Action Plan

The Action Plan is the final step in the self-assessment process. It should include actions already in place or planned over the short, medium and long run for each of the Principles and corresponding indicators. The objective is for stakeholders to determine what collective actions can be taken to improve the aspects of the water governance system that did not reach a satisfactory level of implementation (Figure 2.12).

Figure 2.12. **The concept of the Action Plan**

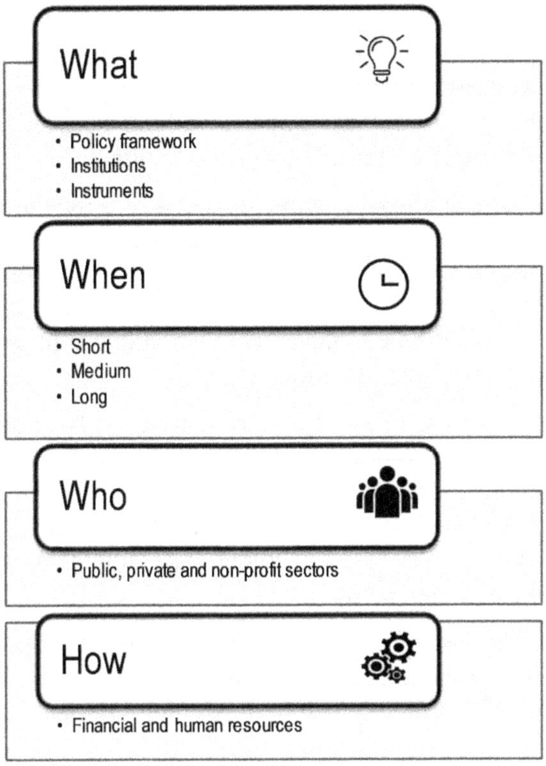

Guidance for end users

This section provides guidance to effectively carry out the self-assessment on the performance of water governance systems against the OECD Principles. The self-assessment exercise aims to ultimately promote a multi-stakeholder dialogue to see what works, what does not and what can be improved in the current water governance system. It therefore seeks to support countries, regions, basins and cities in achieving good water governance to enhance water security and provide better quality services, as foreseen by global frameworks (e.g. SDGs).

The guidance note draws on literature, OECD experience, and the results of the two rounds of pilot tests concerning the application of the indicator framework. The guidance identifies who should carry out the evaluation and how, and what framework conditions are necessary to make self-assessment useful for policy makers and stakeholders. The aim is to avoid a "tick the box" exercise and minimise the risk of consultation capture for a robust evaluation as a basis for improvement.

Framework conditions

There are multiple conditions, outlined below, that need to be met to successfully undertake the self-assessment and identify existing gaps and effective actions for improving water governance systems.

- Make sure that the process is **transparent**. This is needed in all the phases of the process, from the preparatory phase to the discussion of the results. Information should be shared, decisions motivated and discussed, objectives clarified from the beginning of the process. A transparent and open process will enhance trust and commitment for future actions.
- Make sure that the process is **neutral and non-discriminatory**. The lead institution should ensure that stakeholders are heard without prejudice and that their inputs are used for the assessment and beyond without discrimination. Neutrality and independence can be guaranteed by a trusted facilitator.
- Make sure stakeholders **buy-in** to the process and **trust** the lead institution. If the assessment is not fully owned by the leading institution it will be very difficult to take actions based on the results. It is important to establish **ownership** for the self-assessment by explaining Principles and indicators. Stakeholders should be very motivated to contribute to the assessment and also to play a role once actions for improvement have been identified.
- Make sure the process is **open**. It is important to go beyond the "usual suspects" and involve emerging actors and unheard categories, such as women, youth and civil society organisations (Figure 2.14). It is critically important to include also non-water sector civil society organisations that work on governance issues. Established methodologies for stakeholder engagement can help increase the level of understanding and interaction.
- Make sure the process is **forward-looking**. When carrying out the assessment, it is key to think ahead about actions for improvement: who can do what in achieving the goals, when and with what resources (human and financial).

A ten-step assessment

The ten-step assessment provides guidance for carrying out the self-assessment in the preparation phase, during the assessment (diagnosis) and after the assessment (actions). Figure 2.13 and Table 2.8 summarise the steps.

Table 2.8. **Summary table of the key ten-step assessment**

Timeline of the assessment	Assessment phase	Step	Description
Before	Preparation	1	Check roles and responsibilities of the lead institution
		2	Understand the Principles and indicators framework
		3	Set objectives and scope of the assessment
		4	Map stakeholders and their core motivations
		5	Appoint an independent and trusted mentor and facilitator
		6	Agree on the rules of the procedure
During	Diagnosis	7	Organise the multi-stakeholder workshops to assess the water governance system against the traffic light and the checklist, and design the Action Plan
After	Action	8	Link actions to existing policy frameworks, strategies and plans
		9	Set up an accountability process to track progress over time
		10	Consider repeating the assessment in three years' time

Figure 2.13. **A ten-step assessment framework**

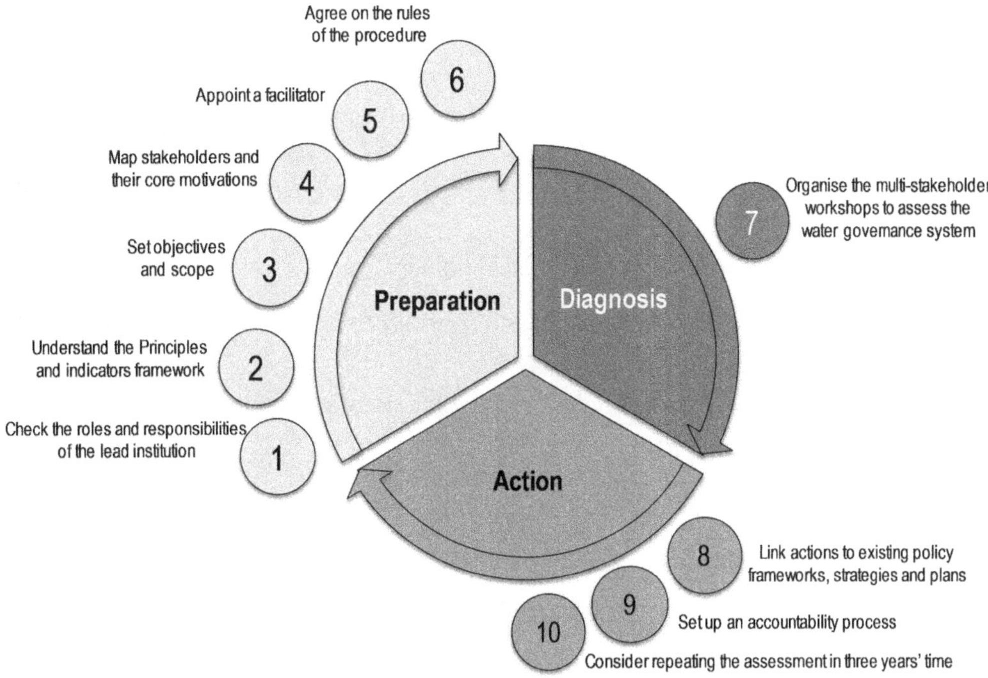

Preparation

Step 1: Check roles and responsibilities of the lead institution. To ensure the highest impact on policy improvement, the lead institution carrying out the assessment should ideally be a public or government authority with water resources or water services management responsibilities. Where this is not possible, the lead institution can be another public, private or non-profit organisation with no conflict of interest to facilitate an unbiased and methodologically sound assessment. In practice, the lead institution should have the convening power to gather stakeholders around the table and to thoughtfully plan and manage the entire evaluation process. In addition to ensuring knowledge and capacity to carry out the assessment, the lead institution should be motivated and able to promote the proposals for change resulting from the review. It would be desirable for the lead institution to have experience in monitoring and assessing water policies, programmes and projects, as well as in the use of methodologies to collect inputs from different stakeholders in a transparent and open way. The lead institution should also take into account the need for human and financial resources to carry out the assessment and organise multi-stakeholder workshops.

Step 2: Understand the Principles and indicators framework. The *OECD Principles on Water Governance* define the key water governance conditions to design and implement effective, efficient and inclusive water policies in a shared responsibility with a broad range of stakeholders. Having a clear understanding of the Principles is the first step for an effective evaluation process. To facilitate this process, the *OECD Principles on Water Governance* have been translated into 16 languages and are available on line. The lead institution should be familiar with the Principles and their corresponding indicators. Once stakeholders are mapped and involved in the process, they need access to available material for the assessment, e.g. Principles, indicators, checklist, guidance and glossary, in order to clarify concepts and definitions, as well as address potential doubts or questions. Stakeholders should be given enough time to understand the Principles and be provided with the necessary support by the lead institution and/or an external mentor.

Step 3: Set objectives and scope of the assessment. There are several objectives that can trigger the assessment of the water governance system in place at national, regional, basin or local level. Generally speaking, the self-assessment is a tool for dialogue among stakeholders on whether existing water institutions, policies and governance instruments are performing well or where adjustments are needed. More specifically, the self-assessment can be carried out in order to:

- promote collective thinking among stakeholders
- share knowledge and address asymmetries of information across governments and stakeholders
- foster learning across stakeholders involved in the water sector;
- raise awareness about the performance or underperformance of the system
- identify deficits in existing policies, institutions and instruments
- develop a critical thinking on who does what and how
- enhance transparency and accountability of water leaders, resulting in increased levels of trust.

It is important to agree collectively on the objectives of the assessment and to discuss their expectations. Hence, the objectives and scope identified by the lead institution can be adjusted after the consultation with stakeholders engaged in the process. Stakeholders should be able to see that their contribution will lead to a concrete output towards the improvement of the current water governance system. Discussing objectives and expectations can help to gauge stakeholder engagement over the long term to address the gaps and actions identified as part of the dialogue. Prior to getting started, the lead institution should also clarify the scope of the assessment, which could concern a specific scale, a specific water function or the water system as a whole, all of the Principles or specific ones.

Step 4: Map stakeholders and their core motivations. The self-assessment should be convened among a minimum level of representatives of several categories of stakeholders, such as: relevant ministries and public agencies across levels of government, different current and potential future categories of water users, water and sanitation utilities, economic and environmental regulators, civil society, scientific organisations/academia, key players from the private sector, donor agencies, financial institutions, etc. (Figure 2.14). Since political will is key to take action after the review, decision makers should be part of the process. For an open debate, it is important to go beyond the "usual suspects" and involve other voices, such as the "under-represented or vulnerable stakeholders" that might be affected by the project/policy process and outcomes and that can influence decisions according to their needs. Box 2.3 discusses the OECD checklist for mapping stakeholders towards inclusive water governance.

Figure 2.14. **Key stakeholders to be engaged in the self-assessment**

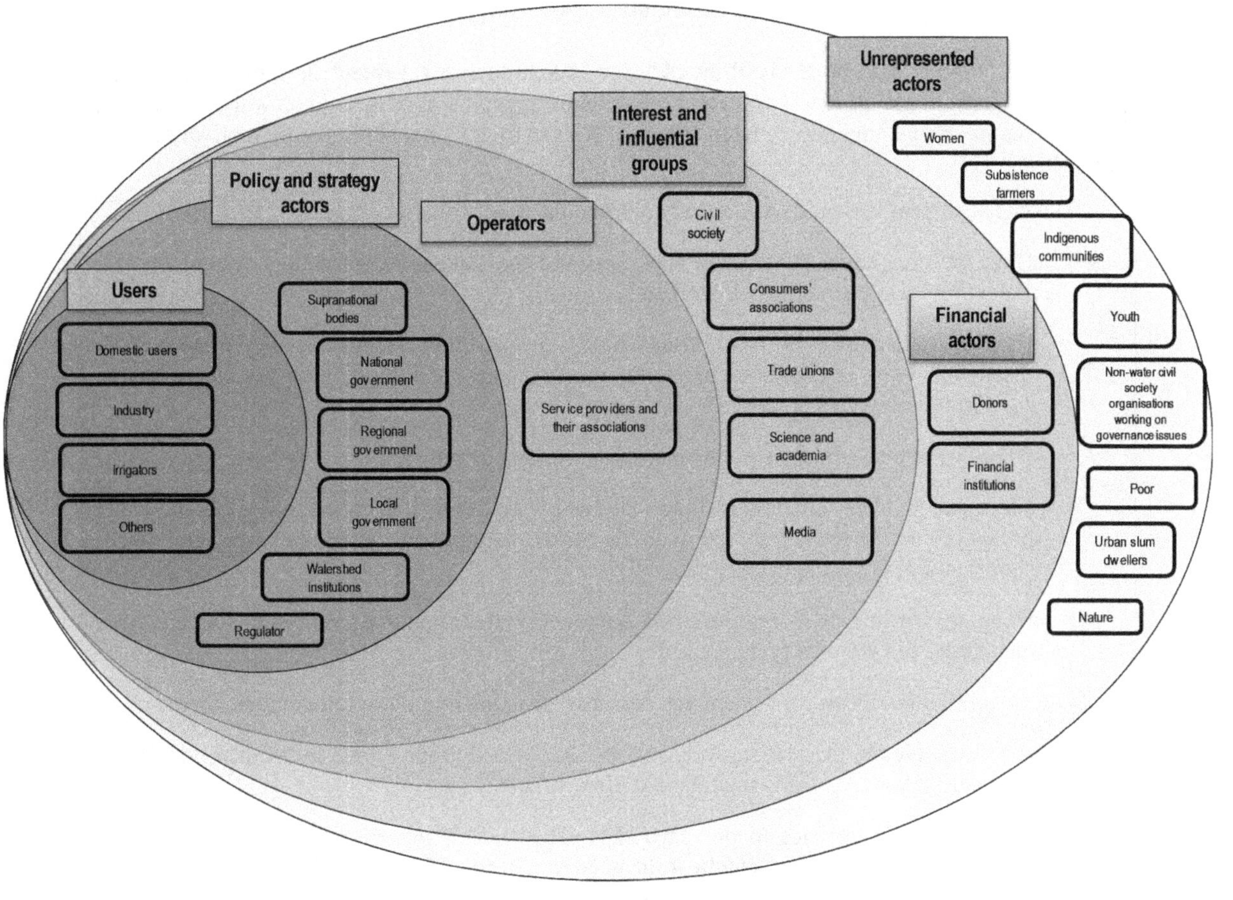

Step 5: **Appoint an independent and trusted facilitator** to work closely with the lead institution throughout the assessment. As facilitator, he/she should guarantee the neutrality of the process and its inclusiveness, ensuring that all the stakeholders are heard, even those less empowered to express their opinions. The independent facilitator should prevent the self-assessment process from turning into a self-satisfaction exercise. The facilitator should also serve as a mentor, guiding the lead institution and stakeholders towards a clear understanding of the Principles and the indicator framework before and during the assessment. The facilitator should be impartial and be recognised as legitimate and credible by all stakeholders involved in the dialogue.

Step 6: Agree on the rules of the procedure. The lead institution should organise a series of workshops lasting a half or full day to share information and opinions, gather data and identify possible ways forward for improving water governance. The workshop discussions should aim to gather views from the full range of stakeholders. Stakeholders will vary in terms of their background, experiences and interests, as well as their level of participation, i.e. some stakeholders may be more vocal than others. The moderator should ensure balanced participation, allowing the stakeholders to pass individual opinions/scores and collectively discuss and dispute the gathered opinions/scores. An example of a participatory assessment tool in the water sector is the Annotated Water Integrity Scan (AWIS) (Box 2.4).

Box 2.3. Guiding questions for an inclusive and equitable multi-stakeholder dialogue

OECD (2015d) developed six Principles for stakeholder engagement in water governance. Principle 1 is about inclusiveness and equity. It calls for mapping all stakeholders who have a stake in the outcome or that are likely to be affected, as well as their responsibility, core motivations and interactions.

The checklist provides guidance to carry out the mapping:

- Have the core water governance functions and the stakeholders formally responsible for executing them been clearly identified?
- Have all stakeholders likely to influence or be impacted by the water policy/project under discussion been engaged, including in other sectors, and those who are likely not to support the measures proposed?
- Are rules in place to allow public dissent or opposing opinions?
- Have stakeholders' interests and motivations been clearly determined as regards the water policy/project under discussion (e.g. demands, aspirations, potential inputs and needs [information, facts, financial resources])?
- Have any institutional/organisational bottlenecks that would prevent stakeholders from engaging been effectively diagnosed?
- Are mitigation measures (incentives, rewards, sanctions) in place to overcome them?
- Are incentives in place to actively involve less-heard groups, such as women, youth and the poor, in water decision making that affects them?
- Are safeguards in place to prevent risks of conflict of interest and/or situations where certain stakeholder groups can be influenced (e.g. through economic incentives)?
- Are the results of stakeholder mappings checked and shared with all those involved and the greater public?

Source: Adapted from OECD (2015d), *Stakeholder Engagement for Inclusive Water Governance*, http://dx.doi.org/10.1787/9789264231122-en.

Diagnosis

Step 7: Organise the multi-stakeholder workshops to assess the water governance system against the traffic light and the checklist, and design the Action Plan. The success of the assessment greatly depends on the familiarity with the concepts expressed by the Principles and indicators, by the variety of stakeholders engaged, and the clarity of the rules. The workshops are the platforms in which stakeholders can confront their opinions and achieve consensus of future activities. Three workshops are considered to be a minimum for an in-depth assessment of the water governance system in place and future changes. They can be organised according to the needs of stakeholders (e.g. by cluster of the Principles, by component of the indicator framework, etc.). Further meetings may be needed depending on the opportunities for stakeholders to provide inputs in between the workshops and to build consensus on the assessment and actions needed. The workshops should consider both the traffic light and the checklist for each of the Principles under assessment. The exercise can cover all of the Principles or a selection of priority Principles according to the stakeholders' needs.

Box 2.4. An example of a multi-stakeholder process: The Annotated Water Integrity Scan

In an Annotated Water Integrity Scan (AWIS) workshop, a trained facilitator enables a constructive dialogue between different stakeholders who may hold differing positions on the issues under review. Participating stakeholders focus on rating and annotating integrity indicators (transparency, accountability and participation) according to simple definitions during a structured workshop. Any AWIS workshop follows a carefully designed process to produce an annotated and consensual overview of the situation in the relevant sub-sector and could be adapted for use with different indicators. The workshop methodology is comprised of the following main steps:

- The AWIS methodology is thoroughly explained to participants to familiarise them with the approach and its intended outcomes.
- Indicators are first rated anonymously by participants. This minimises the risk that some participants may choose to refrain from providing critical opinions because of the prevailing power relations.
- The scores collected from participants are aggregated into average scores, which prevents any particular stakeholder from setting the tone on a given issue and thus yields an impartial score.
- The average scores are shared with the participants, who are then offered an opportunity to provide arguments for both higher and lower scores. This is a crucial step in which stakeholders are encouraged to examine a position even if it is not their own, and provide additional information that can support a rating, whether high or low.
- A second round of anonymous scoring is carried to out to give participants a chance to change their initial position in light of emerging new information.
- Finally, the workshop prompts participants to identify and agree on follow-up actions.

In sum, by following a systematic process that underscores transparency, equity and constructive dialogue, AWIS workshops produce a comprehensive assessment and simultaneously help build trust among different stakeholders to prepare the ground for follow-up action.

Source: Water Integrity Network (2011), "Annotated water integrity scans: A manual to help assess integrity levels in specific sub-sectors of the water sector", www.waterintegritynetwork.net/wp-content/uploads/2015/02/WIN_AWIS_Manual_EN_2011.pdf.

During each workshop:

- Allow time to present and explain the Principles and the indicator framework.
- Discuss, based on material to be shared well in advance of the workshop, the responses to the traffic light and the checklist. Alternatively, if data cannot be collected prior to the workshops, more informed participants may take the lead to start the discussions. If participants do not have access to data or data are lacking prior to the event, stakeholders can use the pre-filled tables (traffic light and checklist) provided by the lead institutions to debate and edit what is reported.
- Clarify any misinterpretations and understand the reasons of drastic diverging opinions, both on the level of implementation of certain governance dimensions and on priorities of actions for the future. Investigating the motivations would help the lead institution, as well as the stakeholders themselves, to analyse the variety of perceptions, which can be due to different levels of knowledge, experiences and interests, or simply to misinterpretation of Principles and indicators. The dialogue would bridge knowledge gaps, if any, and overcome misunderstandings.

- Report on future intents in the Action Plan. This would allow for the identification of priority actions over the short, medium and long term and a discussion on the implementation process, including the role that stakeholders can play.

Action

Step 8: Link actions with the existing policy framework, strategies and plans. The Action Plan can be a useful starting point to identify the concrete means (human, technical and financial resources) needed to put actions into place and to establish a timeline for implementation. It is also a way to reveal the shared responsibilities across public, private and non-profit constituencies to take joint actions for improved governance. The assessment provides an opportunity for different stakeholders to discuss and agree upon what role they will play to implement water policies, alongside policy makers. Actions should be linked to existing policy frameworks, strategies and plans, in order to complement and improve existing tools, rather than necessarily invent new ones.

Step 9: Set up an accountability process to track progress over time and keep the dialogue alive. Keeping the dialogue alive among stakeholders is critical to a strong implementation phase. When possible, the leading institution should provide future opportunities for stakeholders to continue to engage and track progress on their defined objectives. An accountability process should be set up to help facilitate this and verify whether inputs from stakeholders were considered and addressed.

Step 10: Consider repeating the self-assessment every three years. The self-assessment is a static and dynamic exercise to assess current water governance performance and to identify expected changes resulting from targeted actions (e.g. traffic light, Action Plan). After the baseline assessment is complete, an evaluation should be done every three years to assess changes in the governance system. The assessment should take into consideration that stakeholders may change after three years, which could have an impact of the implementation of actions identified during the baseline assessment.

Note

1. Phase II results are available at: www.oecd.org/env/watergovernanceprogramme.htm.

References

Adaptation Fund (2011), "Project level results framework and baseline guideline document", Adaptation Fund, available at: www.oecd.org/env/cc/48332155.pdf.

European Commission (2017), "Indicators to measure social protection performance: Implications for EC programming", *Tools and Methods Series*, Concept Paper No. 5, European Commission, Brussels, https://europa.eu/capacity4dev/t-and-m-series/document/indicators-measure-social-protection-performance.

OECD (2017a), "Draft OECD water governance indicators", OECD Scoping note presented at the 9th OECD Water Governance Initiative Meeting, 3-4 July, Paris.

OECD (2017b), "OECD water governance indicators", document discussed at the 10th OECD Water Governance Iniiative meeting, November, Vienna.

OECD (2017c), "Draft OECD water governance indicators", GOV/RDPC/WGI(2017)1, OECD, Paris.

OECD (2015a), *OECD Principles on Water Governance*, OECD, Paris, www.oecd.org/governance/oecd-principles-on-water-governance.htm.

OECD (2015b), "OECD inventory: Water governance indicators and measurement frameworks", OECD, Paris, https://www.oecd.org/cfe/regional-policy/Inventory_Indicators.pdf.

OECD (2015c), "OECD water governance indictors: OECD scoping note", GOV/RDPC/WGI(2015)7, OECD, Paris.

OECD (2015d), *Stakeholder Engagement for Inclusive Water Governance*, OECD Publishing, Paris, http://dx.doi.org/10.1787/9789264231122-en.

UNDP et al. (2013), "User's guide in assessing water governance", United Nations Development Programme, www.undp.org/content/undp/en/home/librarypage/democratic-governance/oslo_governance_centre/user-s-guide-on-assessing-water-governance.html.

Water Integrity Network (2011), "Annotated water integrity scans: A manual to help assess integrity levels in specific sub-sectors of the water sector", Water Integrity Network, www.waterintegritynetwork.net/wp-content/uploads/2015/02/WIN_AWIS_Manual_EN_2011.pdf.

Annex 2.A1.
Self-assessment tool by Principle

Principle 1: Clear roles and responsibilities

Principle 1: Clear roles and responsibilities

Clearly allocate and distinguish roles and responsibilities for water policy making, policy implementation, operational management and regulation, and foster co-ordination across these responsible authorities.

To that effect, legal and institutional frameworks should:

- Specify the allocation of roles and responsibilities, across all levels of government and water-related institutions in regard to water:
  - policy making, especially priority setting and strategic planning
  - policy implementation, especially financing and budgeting, data and information, stakeholder engagement, capacity development and evaluation
  - operational management, especially service delivery, infrastructure operation and investment
  - regulation and enforcement, especially tariff setting, standards, licensing, monitoring and supervision, control and audit, and conflict management.
- Help identify and address gaps, overlaps and conflicts of interest through effective co-ordination at and across all levels of government.

1.1. Water governance indicators

1.a – WHAT

Existence and level of implementation of a **water law**

Description
This indicator seeks to appraise the existence and level of implementation of a water law, which can be at national level or subnational level depending on the institutional feature of the country (unitary or federal). The law should clearly assign and distinguish water-related roles and responsibilities for policy making (especially priority setting and strategic planning).

1.b – WHO

Existence and functioning of **ministry, line ministry, central agency** with core water-related responsibilities for policy making

Description
This indicator seeks to appraise the existence and functioning of institutions in charge of setting water-related policy goals and strategies and delivering them; these can be at national or subnational level depending on the scale of the self-assessment and the institutional feature of the country (unitary, federal).

1.c – HOW

Existence and implementation of **mechanisms to review roles and responsibilities**, to diagnose gaps and adjust when need be

Description
This indicator seeks to appraise the existence and level of implementation of mechanisms that can help identify areas of water management where there is no clarity on who does what; areas with incoherent and/or contradictory objectives; areas with deficient implementation and/or limited enforcement; and/or areas with overlaps/ duplication of responsibilities. They can take the form of analytical reports, regulatory impact assessments or regulatory reviews; open stakeholder consultations.

1.2. Checklist

- Is there a dedicated water policy, indicating goals, duties, resources needed?

Such a policy can be at national or subnational level depending on the scale at which the assessment is carried out and the constitutional organisation of the country.

- Have applicable **binding and non-binding water-related international or supranational frameworks** and regulations been transposed at national (or subnational) level(s)?
- Are there **horizontal co-ordination mechanisms** across subnational authorities to manage interdependencies for water policy design and implementation?

Examples include inter-municipal or metropolitan collaboration as well as fiscal, financial or other incentives from central/regional governments, specific mechanisms for conflict resolution, joint financing, metropolitan or regional water districts, or informal co-operation around projects.

- Are there **vertical co-ordination mechanisms** or incentives that foster policy alignment, complementarities and co-operation across central and subnational governments?

Examples include contractual arrangements across levels of government; intermediate bodies or actors with core water responsibility; sectoral conferences between central and subnational water players; co-ordination agencies or commissions; shared databases and information systems; financial transfers or incentives; and organisations/tools facilitating the dialogue across levels of government.

Principle 2: Appropriate scales within basin systems

Principle 2: Appropriate scales within basin systems

Manage water at the appropriate scale(s) within integrated basin governance systems to reflect local conditions, and foster co-ordination between the different scales.

To that effect, water management practices and tools should:

- respond to long-term environmental, economic and social objectives with a view to making the best use of water resources, through risk prevention and integrated water resources management
- encourage a sound hydrological cycle management from capture and distribution of freshwater to the release of wastewater and return flows
- promote adaptive and mitigation strategies, action programmes and measures based on clear and coherent mandates, through effective basin management plans that are consistent with national policies and local conditions
- promote multi-level co-operation among users, stakeholders and levels of government for the management of water resources
- enhance riparian co-operation on the use of transboundary freshwater resources.

2.1. Water governance indicators

2.a — WHAT

Existence and level of implementation of **integrated water resources management** policies and strategies

Description

This indicator seeks to appraise the existence and level of implementation of integrated policies and strategies from sub-basin to upper levels to capture and distribute freshwater and to release wastewater and return flows, with a circular economy perspective; to manage water from sources to sea; and to foster conjunctive use and management of surface, groundwater and coastal water(s).

2.b — WHO

Existence and functioning of **institutions managing water at the hydrographic scale**

Description

This indicator seeks to appraise the existence of a basin approach to water management following hydrographic boundaries rather than (only) administrative frontiers. Depending on countries' institutional organisations, such institutions can be decentralised or deconcentrated bodies, catchment-based or catchment-oriented. Besides their existence, the indicator should also appraise the extent to which they carry out their functions related to monitoring, collecting water revenues, co-ordination, regulation, data collection, pollution prevention, issuing water abstraction permits and effluent discharges licences, allocation of uses, planning, assets maintenance and operation, capacity development, public awareness, conflict resolution, and stakeholder engagement. Their activities should be based on basin management plans consistent with national policies and local conditions, defined according to international best practices (for EU member countries, the provisions of the Water Framework Directive could be used as screening criteria).

2.c — HOW

Existence and level of implementation of **co-operation mechanisms** for the management of water resources across water-related users and levels of government from local to basin, regional, national and upper scales

Description

This indicator seeks to appraise the existence and level of implementation of mechanisms to foster co-operation across users, stakeholders and levels of government for the management of water resource. Examples of such mechanisms could include shared data and information system, joint programmes of measure, joint projects or contracts, co-financing, or forms of multi-level dialogue.

2.2. Checklist

- Where they exist, do catchment-based organisations have the adequate level of **autonomy, staff and budget** to carry out their functions?
- Are there policy and economic instruments in place to manage too much, too little and too polluted water at hydrographic scale?

Examples include: river basin plans, water charges, water entitlements, early warning systems for disasters, dedicated water resources funds, models and decision support system, information system, research, development and innovation, inspections, etc.

- In case of **transboundary** rivers, lakes or aquifers, are there **mechanisms or incentives** to co-ordinate among riparian states?

Examples include dedicated commissions, joint basin plans, joint information and/or monitoring systems, mutual assistance programmes, joint research and innovation, early warning and alarm procedures, public participation fora, joint financing and/or cost recovery, dispute resolution mechanisms.

- Are there **co-ordination mechanisms to combine territorial and hydrographic scales** for water resources management, for instance in metropolitan areas?

Examples include multi-sectoral metropolitan bodies, multi-sectoral or bundled utilities for water and related services, rural-urban partnerships, rivers or aquifer contracts, among others.

Principle 3: Policy coherence

Principle 3: Policy coherence

Encourage policy coherence through effective cross-sectoral co-ordination, especially between policies for water and the environment, health, energy, agriculture, industry, spatial planning and land use through:

- encouraging co-ordination mechanisms to facilitate coherent policies across ministries, public agencies and levels of government, including cross-sectoral plans
- fostering co-ordinated management of use, protection and clean-up of water resources, taking into account policies that affect water availability, quality and demand (e.g. agriculture, forestry, mining, energy, fisheries, transportation, recreation and navigation) as well as risk prevention
- identifying, assessing and addressing the barriers to policy coherence from practices, policies and regulations within and beyond the water sector, using monitoring, reporting and reviews
- providing incentives and regulations to mitigate conflicts among sectoral strategies, bringing these strategies into line with water management needs and finding solutions that fit with local governance and norms.

3.1. Water governance indicators

3.a – WHAT

Existence and level of implementation of **cross-sectoral policies and strategies** promoting policy coherence between water and key related areas, in particular environment, health, energy, agriculture, land use and spatial planning

Description
This indicator seeks to appraise the existence and the level of implementation of integrated policies, strategies, fostering coherence across sectors, while minimising contradictory objectives and negative impacts.

3.b – WHO

Existence and functioning of an **inter-ministerial body or institutions for horizontal co-ordination** across water-related policies

Description
This indicator seeks to appraise the existence and functioning of bodies or institutions to facilitate coherent policies across ministries, discussing synergies and managing trade-offs across water, environment, health, energy, agriculture, industry, spatial planning and land use and other relevant areas.

3.c – HOW

Existence and level of implementation of **mechanisms to review barriers to policy coherence** and/or areas where water and related practices, policies or regulations are misaligned

Description
This indicator seeks to appraise the existence and level of implementation of mechanisms to identify barriers that hinder the coherent management of water and key related domains. These could include outdated legislation, distortive subsidies, conflicting interests, competition between ministries, overlapping roles and responsibilities, lack of integrated planning, split incentives or poor enforcement. Examples of such mechanisms include (multi-)sectoral reviews, regulatory impact assessment, inter-ministerial platforms or integrated legislation, among others.

3.2. Checklist

- Is there a **dedicated policy or high-level political support to water management** as a driver to economic growth as featured by the Sustainable Development Goals?
- Are **data and projections on water demanded from agriculture, industry (including energy) and households** available and guiding decisions about handling competing uses now and in the future?
- Is there an **assessment of the distributional impacts on water management** of decisions taken in other areas such as energy subsidies, spatial development, agriculture or environment?
- Are **costs** due to absent/poor water-related policy coherence evaluated and available to decision makers?

Such costs could be economic, social, environmental or financial, or relate to greater risks of human causalities, among others.

- Are **benefits** from policy coherence and policy complementarities evaluated and showcased to decision makers and key stakeholders?

Examples could include reduced information asymmetries, optimisation of financial resources use, reduction/elimination of split incentives/conflicts, equity across users, better disaster preparedness, etc.

- Are there provisions, frameworks or instruments to ensure that decisions taken in other sectors are **water-wise?**

An example would be the water tests whereby any spatial development projects need to feature water-related constraints.

- Are there **horizontal co-ordination mechanisms** at subnational and national levels?

Examples include: cross-sectoral groups/meetings, cross-sectoral policy reviews, financial incentives/conditionalities, joint actions of ministries/agencies at subnational level, cross-sectoral research programmes, etc.

- Are there **conflict mitigation and resolution mechanisms** to manage trade-offs across water-related policy areas?

Examples include top-down or command-and-control mechanisms (water courts, laws, regulations) and bottom-up initiatives (public consultation, stakeholder groups facilitating collaborative solutions, users' associations).

Principle 4: Capacity

> **Principle 4: Capacity**
>
> Adapt the level of capacity of responsible authorities to the complexity of the water challenges to be met, and to the set of competencies required to carry out their duties:
>
> - identifying and addressing capacity gaps to implement integrated water resources management, notably for planning, rule-making, project management, finance, budgeting, data collection and monitoring, risk management and evaluation
> - matching the level of technical, financial and institutional capacity in water governance systems to the nature of problems and needs
> - encouraging adaptive and evolving assignment of competences upon demonstration of capacity, where appropriate
> - promoting the hiring of public officials and water professionals that uses merit-based, transparent processes that are independent from political cycles
> - promoting education and training of water professionals to strengthen the capacity of water institutions as well as stakeholders at large and to foster co-operation and knowledge-sharing.

4.1. Water governance indicators

4.a – WHAT

Existence and level of implementation of hiring policies, based on a **merit-based and transparent professional and recruitment process** of water professionals independent from political cycles

Description
This indicator seeks to appraise the framework conditions (not necessarily water-specific) in place and their level of implementation to assure the presence of competent staff able to deal with technical and non-technical water-related issues across agencies, responsible ministries and water management bodies.

4.b – WHO

Existence and functioning of **mechanisms to identify and address capacity gaps in water institutions**

Description
This indicator seeks to appraise the existence and functioning of mechanisms to identify the level of capacity of responsible authorities in carrying out their duties and coping with water challenges. Duties are: planning, rule-making, project management, finance, budgeting, data collection and monitoring, risk management and evaluation.

4.c – HOW

Existence and level of implementation of **educational and training programmes** for water professionals

Description
This indicator seeks to appraise the existence and level of implementation of capacity-related programmes (e.g. educational curricula, executive training, technical assistance, etc.) to strengthen the capacity of water institutions as well as stakeholders at large in critical areas such as planning, financing and monitoring.

4.2. Checklist

- Are there **incentives** to create water careers in the public sector?
- Are there **guidelines** or standards for capacity building across authorities at all levels?
- Are there **peer-to-peer dialogue platforms** across river basin organisations?
- Are there **networks** of utilities and networks of basin organisations at national level?
- Are institutional strengthening and soft capacity included into **technical assistance programmes**?
- Are there **decentralised co-operation mechanisms** to foster north-south, south-south and north-north experience learning, capacity building and knowledge transfer?

Principle 5: Data and information

Principle 5: Data and information

Produce, update and share timely, consistent, comparable, and policy-relevant water and water-related data and information, and use it to guide, assess and improve water policy, through:

- defining requirements for cost-effective and sustainable production and methods for sharing high-quality water and water-related data and information, e.g. on the status of water resources, water financing, environmental needs, socio-economic features and institutional mapping
- fostering effective co-ordination and experience-sharing among organisations and agencies producing water-related data between data producers and users, and across levels of government
- promoting engagement with stakeholders in the design and implementation of water information systems, and providing guidance on how such information should be shared to foster transparency, trust and comparability (e.g. data banks, reports, maps, diagrams, observatories)
- encouraging the design of harmonised and consistent information systems at the basin scale, including in the case of transboundary water, to foster mutual confidence, reciprocity and comparability within the framework of agreements between riparian countries
- reviewing data collection, use, sharing and dissemination to identify overlaps and synergies and track unnecessary data overload.

5.1. Water governance indicators

5.a

WHAT

Existence and functioning of **updated, timely shared, consistent and comparable water information systems**

Description

This indicator seeks to appraise the existence and functioning of water information systems that can guide decisions and policies related to water. Data could encompass, for instance, the status of water resources, water financing, environmental needs, socio-economic features and institutional mapping.

5.b

WHO

Existence and functioning of public **institutions, organisations and agencies** in charge of producing, co-ordinating and disclosing standardised, harmonised and official water-related statistics

Description

This indicator seeks to appraise the existence and functioning of institutions producing independent data and official water-related statistics at national or subnational level. Selected criteria include whether they are endowed with sufficient resources, if they produce information that is reliable, credible and free from political intervention.

5.c

HOW

Existence and level of implementation of mechanisms to identify and review **data gaps, overlaps and unnecessary overload**

Description

This indicator seeks to appraise the existence and level of implementation of mechanisms to review data collection, use, sharing and dissemination to identify overlaps and synergies and to track unnecessary data overload. They can take the form of reviews, reports, open consultations, among others.

5.2. Checklist

- Are the following data on water and sanitation services available?
  - – service coverage
  - – cost of water services (transporting and supplying water; collecting and treating wastewater; identification of records relating to personnel and equipment)
  - – cost recovery and prices in relation to consumer income and purchasing power
  - – knowledge of assets, maintenance of infrastructure programmes to ensure sustainable operation, maintenance and renewal
  - – drinking water and wastewater quality controls against specified standards.
- Are key data on water services **publicly available and communicated** to customers?
- Is the water supply and sanitation information system **harmonised, integrated, standardised and co-ordinated** across relevant agencies and responsible authorities across relevant governance scales?
- Are the following **data on integrated water resources management** available?
  - – qualitative and quantitative state of resources including hydrogeological data
  - – user registry and entitlement permits for water withdrawal
  - – withdrawals and consumption by sectors (domestic, energy, agriculture, industry)
  - – pollution sources, registry, permits and measurement of quality parameters of pollution emission
  - – hydrological connection between surface water and groundwater resources
  - – water charges collected and subsidies given and their expenditure.
- Are key data on water resources management **publicly available** and communicated to users?
- Is the integrated water resources management water information system **harmonised, integrated, standardised and co-ordinated** across relevant agencies and responsible authorities across relevant governance scales?
- Are the following data on **risk management** available?
  - – projections/scenarios with reference to climate change and exposed lives and goods, risks of floods, drought and accidental pollution
  - – meteorological data, including data on rainfall
  - – data on water flows and pressures and extension of flooded areas for known events
  - – historical data on water disasters
  - – data on vulnerability (human beings and properties)/ exposure to risk.
- Are key data on water risk management **publicly available** and communicated to citizens?
- Is the risk management water information system **harmonised, integrated, standardised and co-ordinated** across relevant agencies and responsible authorities across relevant governance scales?
- Are there **real-time data** and do they guide decision making?
- Are there **bottom-up mechanisms** to produce and disclose water-related data and information in a shared responsibility across levels of government, public, private and non-profit stakeholders?
- Are there **platforms for dialogue** between data producers and users?
- Are there incentives or forms of **co-operation between primary and other data producers**?
- Do **online** platforms/tools/agreements exist for experience and knowledge sharing?
- Do incentives exist to produce, disclose and use **water-related data and information**, through innovative ways?

Examples are big/smart/mobile data, digital maps, real-time sensors and monitoring.

Principle 6: Financing

Principle 6: Financing

Ensure that governance arrangements help mobilise water finance and allocate financial resources in an efficient, transparent and timely manner through:

- promoting governance arrangements that help water institutions across levels of government raise the necessary revenues to meet their mandates, building through, for example, principles such as the polluter-pays and user-pays, as well as payment for environmental services
- carrying out sector reviews and strategic financial planning to assess short-, medium-, and long-term investment and operational needs and take measures to help ensure availability and sustainability of such finance
- adopting sound and transparent practices for budgeting and accounting that provide a clear picture of water activities and any associated contingent liabilities, including infrastructure investment, and aligning multi-annual strategic plans to annual budgets and medium-term priorities of governments
- adopting mechanisms that foster the efficient and transparent allocation of water-related public funds (e.g. through social contracts, scorecards and audits)
- minimising unnecessary administrative burdens related to public expenditure while preserving fiduciary and fiscal safeguards.

6.1. Water governance indicators

6.a — WHAT

Existence and level of implementation of **governance arrangements** that help water institutions collect the necessary revenues to meet their mandates and drive water-sustainable and efficient behaviours

Description

This indicator seeks to appraise the existence and level of implementation of governance arrangements that help water institutions collect the necessary revenues to meet their mandates, based on key principles such as the polluter-pays, user-pays and the interest-pay-say, as well as payment for environmental services.

6.b — WHO

Existence and functioning of **dedicated institutions** in charge of collecting water revenues and allocating them at the appropriate scale

Description

This indicator seeks to appraise the extent to which water management institutions (e.g. utilities, regulators, basin organisations) exist and are in charge of collecting water revenues (taxes and tariffs) and allocating them in a transparent, efficient and timely manner.

6.c — HOW

Existence and level of implementation of mechanisms to assess **short-, medium-, and long-term investment and operational needs** and ensure the availability and sustainability of such finance

Description

This indicator seeks to appraise the existence and level of implementation of mechanisms to identify investment needs and funding gaps in terms of physical infrastructure and governance functions to manage too much, too little, too polluted waters and to sustain/achieve universal coverage of water services. Examples include *ex ante* and *ex post* evaluation (e.g. related to the use of economic instruments), sectoral reviews, economic and affordability studies (e.g. to assess users' capacity or willingness to pay), forecasts and projections, and multi-annual budgeting or planning.

6.2. Checklist

- Are there enough **financial revenues** (taxes, tariffs, transfers) to cover operational costs and long-term assets renewal to protect ecosystems services and to finance biodiversity programmes?
- Is there **standardised/harmonised guidance** at national or subnational level for setting and governing economic instruments such as tariffs, abstraction or pollution charges, groundwater tax?
- Are **abstraction charges** in place to foster water-use efficiency and collect revenues?
- Are **pollution charges** in place to foster water quality management and collect revenues?
- Are there schemes or incentives for **payment for environmental services**?
- Do flexible and **solidarity mechanisms** exist in case of water-related disasters?
- Are there **multi-annual strategic plans** to review short-, medium- and long-term investment needs and support policy continuity?
- Are there **investment plans and programmes** and do they guide decision making?
- Are there **clear budget transparency principles and rules** applied at all levels of government?
- Are there measures to minimise unnecessary **administrative burdens** when collecting and disbursing water-related revenues?
- Are there **reporting mechanisms** and audits of financial administration for water-related expenditure?
- Are there mechanisms or incentives to foster the efficient and transparent **allocation of water-related revenues**?

Examples include: social contracts, scorecards, cost-benefit analyses.

Principle 7: Regulatory frameworks

Principle 7: Regulatory frameworks

Ensure that sound water management regulatory frameworks are effectively implemented and enforced in pursuit of the public interest through:

- ensuring a comprehensive, coherent, and predictable legal and institutional framework that sets rules, standards and guidelines for achieving water policy outcomes, and encourages integrated long-term planning
- ensuring that key regulatory functions are discharged across public agencies, dedicated institutions and levels of government and that regulatory authorities are endowed with the necessary resources
- ensuring that rules, institutions and processes are well co-ordinated, transparent, non-discriminatory, participative, and easy to understand and enforce
- encouraging the use of regulatory tools (evaluation and consultation mechanisms) to foster the quality of regulatory processes and make the results accessible to the public, where appropriate
- setting clear, transparent and proportionate enforcement rules, procedures, incentives and tools (including rewards and penalties) to promote compliance and achieve regulatory objectives in a cost-effective way
- ensuring that effective remedies can be claimed through non-discriminatory access to justice, considering the range of options as appropriate.

7.1. Water governance indicators

7.a

WHAT

Existence and level of implementation of a **sound water management regulatory framework** to foster enforcement and compliance, achieve regulatory objectives in a cost-effective way, and protect the public interest

Description

This indicator seeks to appraise the existence and level of implementation of regulatory frameworks to foster enforcement and compliance, achieve regulatory objectives in a cost-effective way, and protect the public interest. The functioning should take into account their clarity, comprehensiveness, coherence and predictability.

7.b

WHO

Existence and functioning of **dedicated public institutions** responsible for ensuring key regulatory functions for water services and resources management

Description

This indicator seeks to appraise the extent to which: 1) key regulatory functions are entrusted to and carried out by responsible authorities, in particular tariff setting and affordability; standard setting; licensing, monitoring and supervision; control and audit; conflict management; 2) how such institutions perform in carrying out their responsibilities. The indicator deliberately encompasses the entire water cycle (services and resources) and may require trade-offs when building consensus across stakeholders as some institutions may perform better than others depending on the water management function,

7.c

HOW

Existence and level of implementation of **regulatory tools to foster the quality of regulatory processes** for water management at all levels

Description

This indicator seeks to appraise the existence and level of implementation of regulatory tools - such as evaluation and consultation mechanisms - to ensure that rules, institutions and processes are fit-for-purpose, well co-ordinated, cost-effective, transparent, non-discriminatory, participative, easy to understand and to enforce.

7.2. Checklist

- Is there a systematic requirement to consider existing **international standards and norms** in the development and revision of national and/or subnational legal frameworks?
- Are there a **dedicated regulatory agency(ies)/bodies or capacities (e.g. within a ministry)** in charge of enforcement and compliance for water resources, water services and disaster risk management?
- When they exist are regulatory agencies **subject to by laws or internal regulations** that clearly state their mandate and powers?
- Are relevant regulatory and inspection authorities embedded with resources in line with their mandate? In case of dedicated regulatory agency(ies), are they **financially independent**?
- Do regulatory authorities take decisions that can also be legally binding?
- Are evaluation **mechanisms in place** to systematically and regularly performance/effectiveness, gaps and overlaps in the regulatory framework?

For instance, areas with regulatory vacuum/gaps, incoherent and/or contradictory objectives, deficient implementation and/or limited enforcement, overlaps/duplication of responsibilities, lack of consistency and continuity of regulation, etc.

- Are water-related legislations subject to **regulatory impact assessment**?
- Are there **reviews** of the governance and performance of regulatory and inspection agencies or bodies?
- Are there water-specific **inspectors** (e.g. a water "police") or other specific enforcement tools in place?
- Are there **co-ordination instruments** between water relevant ministries and bodies?
- Are there **requirements to disclose information** and inputs used for regulatory decisions?
- Can regulatory decisions taken be repealed?
- Are there mechanisms to solve **water-related disputes** (be they water-specific or not)?
- Where **self-regulation** mechanisms exist, are they object of regular performance assessment?

Principle 8: Innovative governance

Principle 8: Innovative governance

Promote the adoption and implementation of innovative water governance practices across responsible authorities, levels of government and relevant stakeholders:

- encouraging experimentation and pilot testing on water governance, drawing lessons from successes and failures, and scaling up replicable practices
- promoting social learning to facilitate dialogue and consensus-building, for example through networking platforms, social media, information and communication technologies and user-friendly interfaces (e.g. digital maps, big data, smart data and open data) and other means
- promoting innovative ways to co-operate, pool resources and capacity, build synergies across sectors and search for efficiency gains, notably through metropolitan governance, inter-municipal collaboration, urban-rural partnerships and performance-based contracts
- promoting a strong science-policy interface to contribute to better water governance and bridge the divide between scientific findings and water governance practices.

8.1. Water governance indicators

8.a – WHAT

Existence and level of implementation of **policy frameworks and incentives fostering innovation** in water management practices and processes

Description
This indicator seeks to appraise the existence and level of implementation of policy and regulatory incentives that foster water-related innovation in terms of products, institutional and contractual design, and governance processes. Examples include frameworks that can incentivise experimentation or pilots to draw lessons and share experience prior to generalising a given reform or process at a larger scale; incentives for innovative financing; incentives for the use of alternative water sources, etc.

8.b – WHO

Existence and functioning of **institutions encouraging bottom-up initiatives, dialogue and social learning as well as experimentation in water management at different levels**

Description
This indicator seeks to appraise the existence and functioning of institutions encouraging water governance innovation and responding to new needs for water governance practices. They could be in charge of promoting innovative ways to co-operate across government and stakeholders, pool resources and upscale water governance innovation.

8.c – HOW

Existence and level of implementation of **knowledge- and experience-sharing mechanisms** to bridge the divide between science, policy and practice

Description
This indicator seeks to appraise the existence and level of implementation of knowledge- and experience-sharing instruments to foster the science-policy interface, such as multi-stakeholder co-creation processes and tools supporting decision-making processes based on scientific evidence, communicated for example through interactive maps, simulation models, etc.

8.2. Checklist

- Are there any **public bodies or accredited bodies** fostering innovation (financing, sharing feedback, assessing, incentivising)?
- Do innovative **tools and processes** exist to:
  - build capacities
  - raise awareness
  - engage stakeholders
  - share information
  - engage within and across organisations?
- Are **information and communication technologies** used to guide better public action in water management and how?
- Are there **reviews** to evaluate the state of play of and potential for technical and non-technical innovation, costs/benefits of innovation, as well as regulations and standards hindering innovation?
- Do **platforms** exist to draw lessons from failures in water policy and governance, and to catalyse and scale-up best practices and success stories?
- Are there innovative **co-operation mechanisms** across territories and water users?

Examples include metropolitan governance, inter-municipal collaboration, urban-rural partnerships, performance-based contracts.

Principle 9: Integrity and transparency

Principle 9: Integrity and transparency

Mainstream integrity and transparency practices across water policies, water institutions and water governance frameworks for greater accountability and trust in decision making through:

- promoting legal and institutional frameworks that hold decision makers and stakeholders accountable, such as the right to information and independent authorities to investigate water-related issues and law enforcement
- encouraging norms, codes of conduct or charters on integrity and transparency in national or local contexts and monitoring their implementation
- establishing clear accountability and control mechanisms for transparent water policy making and implementation; diagnosing and mapping on a regular basis existing or potential drivers of corruption and risks in all water-related institutions at different levels, including for public procurement
- adopting multi-stakeholder approaches, dedicated tools and action plans to identify and address water integrity and transparency gaps (e.g. integrity scans/pacts, risk analysis, social witnesses).

9.1. Water governance indicators

9.a — WHAT

Existence and level of implementation of **legal and institutional frameworks** (not necessarily water-specific) on integrity and transparency which also apply to water management at large

Description

This indicator seeks to appraise the existence and level of implementation of legal and institutional frameworks that hold decision makers and stakeholders accountable (e.g. public procurement), and whereby the public interest can be safeguarded, malpractices can be identified and sanctioned, and effective remedies can be claimed. Examples include the right to information, public procurement, in accordance with best international practice, as well as the transposition of applicable international conventions.

9.b — WHO

Existence and functioning of **independent courts** (not necessarily water-specific) **and supreme audit institutions** that can investigate water-related infringements and safeguard the public interest

Description

This indicator seeks to appraise the existence and functioning of independent authorities and audit institutions (be they water-specific or not) to investigate water-related infractions through inspections and controls, enact sanctions in case of violation. Selected criteria for assessment include the effectiveness, capacity, independence and accessibility of such institutions.

9.c — HOW

Existence and level of implementation of **mechanisms** (not necessarily water-specific) **to identify potential drivers of corruption and risks in all water-related institutions** at different levels, as well as other water integrity and transparency gaps

Description

This indicator seeks to appraise the existence and the level of implementation of mechanisms that can diagnose, discourage and/or prevent poor transparency and integrity practices at different levels. Examples include integrity scans, multi-stakeholder approaches, social witnesses, social monitoring (e.g. to track consumer perceptions and petty corruption in water management), auditable anti-corruption plans, risk analysis and risk maps.

9.2. Checklist

- When roles and responsibilities for water supply and sanitation service delivery, water resources management, or disaster risk reduction are delegated to dedicated public or private entities, are there **contractual arrangements** between organising and executive bodies?
- Are relevant **international conventions, resolutions or frameworks** related to transparency and integrity transposed into national legislation?
- Are there institutional **anti-corruption plans**, **codes of conduct** or charters?
- Are executive, legislative and judiciary **powers** clearly **separated?**
- Are there provisions for **whistle-blower protection** in legal and institutional frameworks? Are **whistle-blower policies** internalised within all public water sector organisations?
- Are **corruption risks** and actual corruption in the water sector (e.g. manipulation of knowledge and information, bribery, extortion) diagnosed?
- Are there evaluation tools to track **budget transparency** in the water sector?

For instance the Open Budget Index of the International Budget Partnership

- Are water accounts separated to ensure **traceability** of the water money?
- Are there **evaluation tools** to track reporting on nepotisms and graft; evasion of rules and regulations; political capture; fraud; unethical practices, including those linked with petty corruption manipulated accounting; bad corporate management?

Examples of petty corruption are. illegal connections, fraudulent metering and billing, etc.

- Are there mechanisms/tools to track **transparency, accountability and participation** in the water sector?

Examples include. reviews of service providers' performance, water-related public expenditure reports, corporate reporting on the implementation of anti-corruption plans, etc.

- Are there mechanisms to assess the **economic, social and environmental costs of water-related corruption?**

Examples include integrity scans, integrity risk assessments, independent investigations including by the media.

- Are there **processes and/or platforms** for dialogue on the **drivers** to corruption and malpractices?
- Are there **requirements in place for regular financial disclosure** of assets, income and interests?
- Are **anti-bribery management systems** in place?

For instance the ISO 37001: 2016.

Principle 10: Stakeholder engagement

Principle 10: Stakeholder engagement

Promote stakeholder engagement for informed and outcome-oriented contributions to water policy design and implementation through:

- mapping public, private and non-profit actors who have a stake in the outcome or who are likely to be affected by water-related decisions, as well as their responsibilities, core motivations and interactions
- paying special attention to under-represented categories (youth, the poor, women, indigenous people, domestic users) newcomers (property developers, institutional investors), and other water-related stakeholders and institutions
- defining the line of decision making and the expected use of stakeholders' inputs, and mitigating power imbalances and risks of consultation capture from over-represented or overly vocal categories, as well as between expert and non-expert voices
- encouraging capacity development of relevant stakeholders as well as accurate, timely and reliable information, as appropriate
- assessing the process and outcomes of stakeholder engagement to learn, adjust and improve accordingly, including the evaluation of costs and benefits of engagement processes
- promoting legal and institutional frameworks, organisational structures and responsible authorities that are conducive to stakeholder engagement, taking account of local circumstances, needs and capacities
- customising the type and level of stakeholder engagement to the needs and keeping the process flexible to adapt to changing circumstances.

10.1. Water governance indicators

10.a – WHAT

Existence and level of implementation of **legal frameworks to engage stakeholders** in the design and implementation of water-related decisions, policies and projects

Description

This indicator seeks to appraise the existence and level of implementation of legal frameworks to engage stakeholders in water-related decision making. In all cases, they should discourage consultation capture and consultation fatigue through balanced representativeness as well as clarity and accountability on the expected use of stakeholders' inputs.

10.b – WHO

Existence and functioning of **organisational structures and responsible authorities** to engage stakeholders in water-related policies and decisions

Description

This indicator seeks to appraise the existence and functioning of dedicated stakeholder engagement institutions or platforms, such as catchment-based authorities, decentralised assemblies, governing boards, national or subnational water councils or committees, as well as more informal forms of community-based engagement. A list of such mechanisms/institutions is available in OECD (2015), *Stakeholder Engagement for Inclusive Water Governance* (Chapter 5), and could be used as a basis.

10.c – HOW

Existence and level of implementation of **mechanisms to diagnose and review stakeholder engagement** challenges, processes and outcomes

Description

This indicator seeks to appraise the existence and level of implementation of mechanisms to diagnose prominent obstacles, challenges or risks such as consultation capture, consultation fatigue or lack of resources (capacity and funding), but also processes and outcomes. This is important in order to learn, adjust and improve accordingly, including the evaluation of costs and benefits of engagement processes. Examples include satisfaction surveys, benchmarks, impact assessment, financial analysis, evaluation reports or multi-stakeholder workshops/meetings. Further details on such evaluation mechanisms can be found in Chapter 7 of OECD (2015), *Stakeholder Engagement for Inclusive Water Governance*.

10.2. Checklist

- Is the **Arhus Convention** and/or other legal and institutional frameworks for stakeholder engagement adopted?
- Was a stakeholder **mapping** carried out to make sure that all those who have a stake in the outcome or that are likely to be affected are clearly identified, and their responsibilities, core motivations and interactions understood?
- Are the ultimate **line of decision making**, the **objectives** of stakeholder engagement and the expected **use of inputs** clearly defined?
- Are there mechanisms or regular assessments of stakeholder engagement **costs or obstacles** at large?
- Is needed **information** for result-oriented stakeholder engagement **shared**?
- Is the type and level of engagement **customised** and the process flexible to adjust to changing circumstances?
- Is there a national **multi-stakeholder co-ordination platform** including representatives from public, private and non-profit sectors and different categories of users?
- Are there mechanisms in place to engage **science in decision making?**
- Are there **formal and informal mechanisms** to engage stakeholders?
- Do tailored **communication strategies** exist for relevant stakeholders, including the general public, regarding all aspects of water management?

Principle 11: Trade-offs across users, rural and urban areas, and generations

Principle 11: Trade-offs across users, rural and urban areas, and generations

Encourage water governance frameworks that help manage trade-offs across water users, rural and urban areas, and generations, through:

- promoting non-discriminatory participation in decision making across people, especially vulnerable groups and people living in remote areas
- empowering local authorities and users to identify and address barriers to access quality water services and resources and promoting rural-urban co-operation, including through greater partnership between water institutions and spatial planners
- promoting public debate on the risks and costs associated with too much, too little or too polluted water to raise awareness, build consensus on who pays for what, and contribute to better affordability and sustainability now and in the future
- encouraging evidence-based assessment of the distributional consequences of water-related policies on citizens, water users and places to guide decision making.

11.1. Water governance indicators

11.a — WHAT

Existence and level of implementation of formal provisions or legal frameworks fostering **equity** across water users, rural and urban areas, and generations

Description

This indicator seeks to appraise the existence and functioning of provisions and frameworks fostering equity across users, rural and urban areas and generations. Equity can be understood in terms of outcomes (to ensure that costs and benefits are distributed fairly) as well as in terms of processes (to ensure that water users are treated fairly). Such frameworks should incentivise non-discriminatory participation in decision-making across people, especially vulnerable groups and people living in remote areas, promote rural-urban linkages, and minimise social, financial and environmental liabilities on future generations. Examples of such frameworks include the effective transposition of international binding and non-binding regulations or soft law that the country may be subject to (e.g. human right to drinking water and sanitation, sustainable development goals, new urban agenda) as well as other forms of incentives.

11.b — WHO

Existence and functioning of an **Ombudsman or institution(s)** to protect water users, including vulnerable groups

Description

This indicator seeks to appraise the existence and functioning of an Ombudsman or dedicated institutions (not necessarily water-specific) protecting vulnerable groups, mediating disputes, addressing users complaints and managing trade-offs when need be.

11.c — HOW

Existence and implementation of **mechanisms or platforms to manage trade-offs across users, territories and/or over time in a non-discriminatory, transparent and evidence-based manner**

Description

This indicator seeks to appraise the existence and level of implementation of mechanisms or platforms to promote non-discriminatory, transparent and evidence-based decision making on trade-offs needed across people, time and places. This could include public debates and rural-urban co-operation (partnerships, projects, etc.).

11.2. Checklist

- Are there requirements/frameworks for **prioritisation among water uses in case of scarcity or emergency situations**?
- Are there **explicit measures** in place to identify access to water services by vulnerable groups, such as First Nation communities, refugees, economic migrants and the homeless?
- Are **rural-urban linkages** clearly identified and addressed in water management?
- Are there **social tariffs or other measures** for vulnerable categories of water users?
- Are the **capacity to pay** and **willingness to pay** of water users evaluated through solid economic analysis and dedicated surveys?
- Are analyses for **supporting decision making** carried out in case of conflicting objectives across users, or geographical/social disparities in accessing water resources and services? (e.g. multi-criteria decision analysis, cost-benefit analysis).

Principle 12: Monitoring and evaluation

Principle 12: Monitoring and evaluation

Promote regular monitoring and evaluation of water policy and governance where appropriate, share the results with the public and make adjustments when needed:

- promoting dedicated institutions for monitoring and evaluation that are endowed with sufficient capacity, the appropriate degree of independence and resources as well as the necessary instruments
- developing reliable monitoring and reporting mechanisms to effectively guide decision making
- assessing to what extent water policy fulfils the intended outcomes and water governance frameworks are fit-for-purpose
- encouraging timely and transparent sharing of the evaluation results and adapting strategies as new information becomes available.

12.1. Water governance indicators

12.a — WHAT

Existence and level of implementation of policy frameworks promoting regular **monitoring and evaluation** of water policy and governance

Description
This indicator seeks to appraise the existence and functioning of frameworks promoting regular monitoring and evaluation of water policy and governance, in order to effectively guide decision making.

12.b — WHO

Existence and functioning of **institutions in charge of monitoring and evaluation of water policies** and practices and help adjust where need be

Description
This indicator seeks to appraise the existence and functioning of monitoring institutions (not necessarily water-specific) that are endowed with sufficient capacity, resources, autonomy and legitimacy to produce evidence-based assessment on the performance of water management and governance and support decision making accordingly. Such institutions should be independent from political interference, at arm's length from water managers and accountable for the outcomes of their evaluation and monitoring.

12.c — HOW

Existence and level of implementation of **monitoring and evaluation mechanisms** to measure to what extent water policy fulfils the intended outcomes and water governance frameworks are fit-for-purpose

Description
This indicator refers to mechanisms such as: *ex post* evaluations, as well as water governance reviews, national assessments, etc.

12.2. Checklist

- Do **formal requirements** exist for **evaluation and monitoring**?
- Are there agreed-upon **key performance indicators**?
- Do monitoring and reporting **mechanisms** exist?

Examples are joint sector reviews, surveys/polls, benchmarking, evaluation reports, ex post *financial analysis, regulatory tools, national observatories, parliamentary consultations, etc.*

- Are there **provisions or incentives** for civil society monitoring?
- Are there **financial resources** available train civil society organisations in project monitoring?
- Are the **results** of the monitoring and evaluation process shared with the wider public?
- Does a **national co-ordination** platform or alike produce evaluation and monitoring reports for parliamentarian discussion on water issues?

Chapter 3.

Evolving practices on water governance

This chapter provides 54 examples of evolving water governance practices that document the implementation of the OECD Principles on Water Governance. *It guides the reader through what makes water governance improve in practice and how to foster peer-to-peer dialogue and bench learning across cities, basins and countries facing similar types of water governance challenges. The chapter provides lessons learnt at various levels (local, basin, national) as well as for policy frameworks, institutions and policy instruments, and could help with future implementation of the OECD Principles.*

The statistical data for Israel are supplied by and under the responsibility of the relevant Israeli authorities. The use of such data by the OECD is without prejudice to the status of the Golan Heights, East Jerusalem and Israeli settlements in the West Bank under the terms of international law."

Rationale for learning from evolving practices

A way forward to support the implementation of the *OECD Principles on Water Governance* is to identify, collect and scale-up practices that can help governments and stakeholders move from vision to action. Practices illustrate how OECD countries and non-OECD economies have designed and implemented effective, efficient and inclusive water governance systems. They are meant to be replicable and support bench learning across different stakeholders within cities, regions, basins and countries.

Practices help policy makers, practitioners and other stakeholders learn from each other and identify pitfalls to avoid when designing and implementing water policies. Learning from evolving water governance practices is about gaining insights from real examples, looking at what works (or has worked) and seeing how others have dealt with challenges. It can also be about learning what does not work, and what successful stakeholders do differently. Practices can showcase accomplishments and highlight results and lessons learnt that can inspire similar cases.

Stakeholders' needs for evolving practices

An online survey was conducted in 2016 by the OECD Secretariat to scope the expectations and needs of decision makers and stakeholders when searching for practices and case studies on water governance. The objective was to ensure that the work on evolving practices does not duplicate what already exists; is relevant to end users from a policy, decision making and practitioner perspective; and is sufficiently pragmatic and accessible to serve the purpose at the least cost. The results of the survey were used to shape the process (of collecting practices), the content (of practices) and the final output (online format). The survey included ten multiple-choice, ranking and open-ended questions. In all, 164 responses were collected, mostly from representatives of academia, civil society and central governments. The least represented categories of stakeholders were regulators, donors and business.

The survey revealed that there is a high demand for practices to inform decision-making processes. In total, 95% of the respondents noted that they "always" or "sometimes" refer to existing practices/cases to help their decisions and policy choices related to water. A large part of respondents indicated that their main reasons for searching for practices and cases were to access new ideas (68%), looking for solutions to a given problem (54%) and filling a knowledge gap (54%) (Figure 3.1). Respondents also indicated that they most often ask their colleagues (56%) or search online (54%) to find practices. A smaller share of respondents mentioned consulting their institutions' own databases of practices (35%) or reaching out to their peers on social media (24%) as ways to find relevant cases (Figure 3.2). Some respondents encounter difficulties when looking for practices because they struggle to find relevant or helpful cases (19%). For others, it is difficult to apply good practices to their situation, practices are not well documented, or they lack the time to search through large databases (7%).

Results from the survey also indicate that a majority of respondents are most interested in practices and cases that come from their peers, i.e. similar institutions, colleagues, etc. (63%), as well as from stakeholders with whom they engage (e.g. customers, civil society, academics, business, etc.) (Figure 3.3). There is also a strong interest in practices from multiple stakeholders that offer different types of perspectives on a given situation (54%). A smaller share of respondents signalled being interested in practices from other sectors than their own (22%).

Figure 3.1. **Needs of users searching about water governance practices/cases**

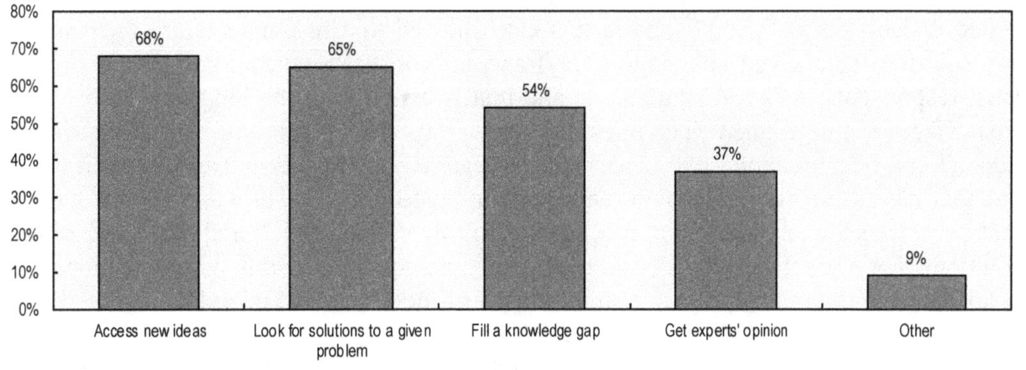

Note: Out of a total of 164 respondents

Source: OECD (2016b), "What do you look for when searching for best practices and case studies on water governance?", survey.

Figure 3.2. **Vehicles used by end users searching for water governance practices/cases**

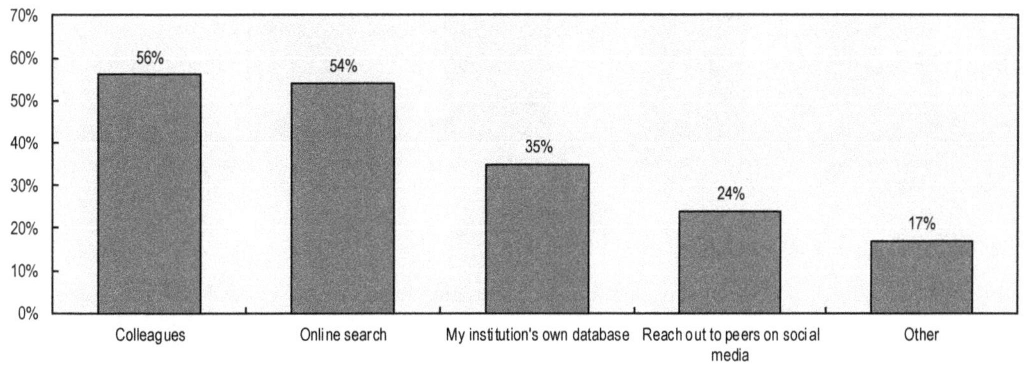

Note: Out of a total of 164 respondents

Source: OECD (2016b), "What do you look for when searching for best practices and case studies on water governance?", survey.

Figure 3.3. **End users' preferred source of practices/cases on water governance**

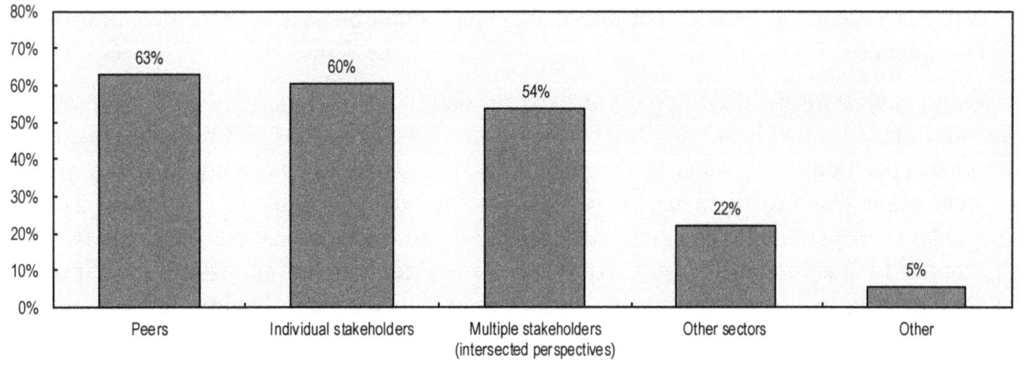

Note: Out of a total of 164 respondents

Source: OECD (2016b), "What do you look for when searching for best practices and case studies on water governance?", survey.

Results showed that most respondents (66%) look for evolving practices (Figure 3.4). To a lesser degree, 44% of decision makers and stakeholders want these practices to be vetted or labelled as "good". The results also showed that respondents are interested in any solutions to a given challenge (37%) and in world-renowned solutions (35%). For most respondents, a "good" practice is one that is efficient in the long term; affordable, cost-effective and funded (i.e. does not only rely on "good will" or "free time"); replicable and "actionable" and consensual as regards the impacts and successes; it is also one that has an impact on demand management, protection of nature and service quality; that empowers stakeholders; that reaches beyond the "water box"; and that leads to new solutions. For a practice to be considered "good", respondents said it should be monitored at all stages of the policy/project in order to be well-documented and evidence-based.

Figure 3.4. **Type of practice or cases on water governance that users mostly search for**

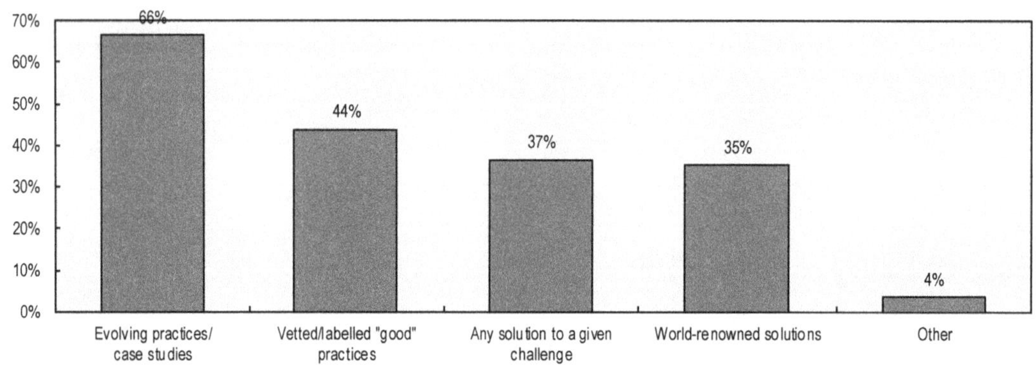

Note: Out of a total of 164 respondents

Source: OECD (2016b), "What do you look for when searching for best practices and case studies on water governance?", survey.

The most important background information respondents look for relates to lessons learnt from failure (56%), followed by the water function concerned (e.g. water services or water resources, etc.) and evidence of impact on water governance and policy outcomes (52% for both). Lessons learnt from success come fourth. Noteworthy is the rather low score for information expected on the provider of the practice (31% of respondents considered it only "somewhat important"), the timeline of the practice (considered by 29% of respondents as "somewhat important") and available links for further information on the practices.

Key shortcomings identified from existing databases include (Figure 3.5): practices are not detailed enough (47%); databases are not user-friendly (32%); difficulty to find practices specifically on water governance (31%); and practices are not assessed against an evaluation framework that qualify them as "good" or "best" (30%). Only 22% of respondents considered the fact that practices are not reviewed by experts as a shortcoming. Respondents identified other downsides, including different definitions across databases for "water governance"; a lack of evidence on stakeholders' appropriation of a given practice; scientifically sound information provided that is not policy relevant; and insufficient data to accompany practice examples.

Figure 3.5. **Shortcomings of existing practice databases on water governance**

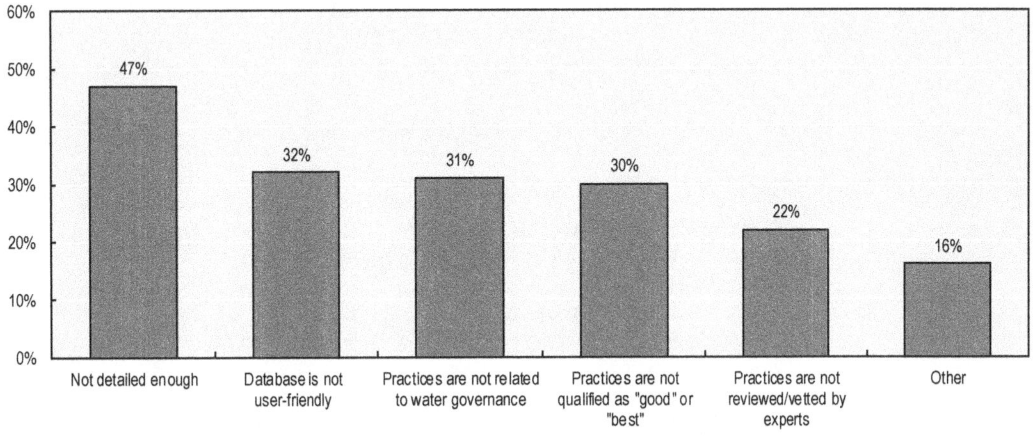

Note: Out of a total of 164 respondents

Source: OECD (2016b), "What do you look for when searching for best practices and case studies on water governance?", survey.

Respondents were asked to identify the most important information they look for when searching for practices related to the 12 OECD Principles. Fifty-one per cent of respondents reported that Principle 8 on regulatory frameworks was "most important", followed by Principle 3 on policy coherence (45%), Principle 12 on monitoring and evaluation (45%), and Principle 1 on roles and responsibilities (45%). Principle 11 on trade-offs and Principle 5 on data and information were considered "somewhat important" by 18% and 22% of respondents respectively.

Respondents also pointed out existing information gaps and transferability issues with some practices. These gaps relate mainly to the context (legal, economic, social, cultural, hydrological), the resources required (whether human, financial and skills/capacities), and the main drivers of the practices (e.g. water pollution, water-related disasters, competition across water users, etc.). Respondents also noted that they would like to consult databases proposing a dynamic analysis of practices that span the entire process, including the *ex post* stage, with more insights on the ownership of a given project or reforms by the various stakeholder involved. In addition, respondents stated that testimonies from the field (i.e. users' and stakeholders' views), information to support a business case for using new strategies as well as on the process-based outcomes of the practices would be useful. According to respondents, the databases should provide more information on the sustainability and transferability of practices as well as how they relate to broader governance challenges in the area concerned and to the Sustainable Development Goals.

Highlights from a review of existing online databases

A preliminary step to developing a set of evolving practices was to inventory existing solutions and case studies (Table 3.1). The inventory was conducted in October and November 2016, and highlighted the strengths and weaknesses of 23 online databases focusing on water governance or water management. This process sought to assess the databases to best determine how to fill any information gaps. The exercise demonstrated that none of the existing databases cover water governance as articulated in the 12 OECD Principles, and they do not include lessons learnt. The results concluded that there would be value added in collecting practices to: 1) assist decision makers and stakeholders with their implementation efforts; 2) help them save money, time and effort by learning from mistakes made by others; 3) adopt proven strategies to improve their probability of success; 4) learn about other projects conducted within their field and region to co-ordinate efforts; and 5) provide a source from which to draw case studies for presentations and training.

Table 3.1. **Inventory of relevant online databases on water**

Water-specific databases	– "Water for Life" UN-Water Best Practice Award website – UN Water and Sanitation Best Practices Platform – Solutions for Water Platform – 6th World Water Forum – GWP IWRM Toolbox – IWMI Success Stories webpage – Euro-Mediterranean information system on know-how in the water sector – WaterLex Toolbox – Restoring Europe's Rivers – Water Action Hub project database – CEO Water Mandate – Geneva Water Hub – Every Drop Matters projects – CAWSI California Agricultural Water Stewardship Initiative – Water Toolbox US – Water Integrity Network – Danubis Utility Database – Interregional Europe Programme Good Practices database – Reform restoring rivers for effective catchment management – Associated Programme on Flood Management (APFM) – Natural Water Retention Measures (NWRM) – Bottom-up climate adaptation strategies towards a sustainable Europe (BASE) – European Climate Adaptation Platform – OpenNESS case studies – DESSIN – AQUACROSS – Infoportal Trinkwasser (available in German only) – WasserWerk (available in German only) – Aktiv für unser Wasser (available in German only)
Non-water-specific databases	– GOVLAB – Engagement Platform on Localizing the SDGs – OECD Public Procurement Toolbox – Energy Efficient Cities Case Studies Database – Equator Initiative: A Partnership for Resilient Communities – Seeds of good anthropocene – National League of Cities' Sustainable Cities platform – ECONADAPT – OPERA: Ecosystem Science for Policy and Practice

Source: OECD (2016a), "OECD inventory of best practices databases", unpublished.

The inventory process provided good insight into what kinds of evolving practices should be collected and shared across stakeholder groups. It highlighted that examples should have a sound narrative, clearly outlining the learning process and focusing on how to put water governance into practice, while making clear distinctions between water governance challenges, opportunities for improved governance, suggested measures to enhance governance and intended outcomes. To be effective, examples should be presented in a concise way, including relevant details that are useful to the range of end users (e.g. regulators, business, etc.). This requires striking a balance between descriptive and analytical information by having access to the meta-information on the practice in a short paragraph and/or with data visualisation, but also by providing the opportunity to get additional information.

A set of evolving practices on water governance

The set of 54 evolving water governance practices (Table 3.2) is the result of a bottom-up process within the OECD Water Governance Initiative (WGI), a platform of more than 130 members from the public, private and not-for-profit sectors, meeting twice a year since 2013 to share knowledge, experience and best practices on water governance. It encompasses a diverse set of contexts that vary in terms of geographical reach, scale, time frame, actors involved and water functions. These practices are diverse, provide a wealth of information of how water governance works in practice and represent a sound basis for discussions. Table 3.2 groups the evolving practices under the most relevant(s) OECD Principle(s) referenced in each example. While this clustering is not optimal given that several practices are cross-cutting, it sheds light on the most prominent governance dimension emphasised by each practice.

Overview of the set of evolving practices

All relevant water functions (integrated water resources management [IWRM], water quality and sanitation, safe drinking water, water-related disasters) are represented throughout the 54 evolving practices. At least 70% of the examples relate to "water resources" and "sanitation and water quality", close to 60% of the practices deal with "drinking water supply", and around 30% are associated with "water-related disasters" (Figure 3.6). Most of the examples (45 evolving practices) refer to multiple water functions, e.g. 29 of the 31 practices that deal with safe drinking water function also refer to water quality and sanitation, and 15 of the 16 practices that talk about water-related disasters function also related to IWRM.

Figure 3.6. **Share of evolving practices on water governance by water function**

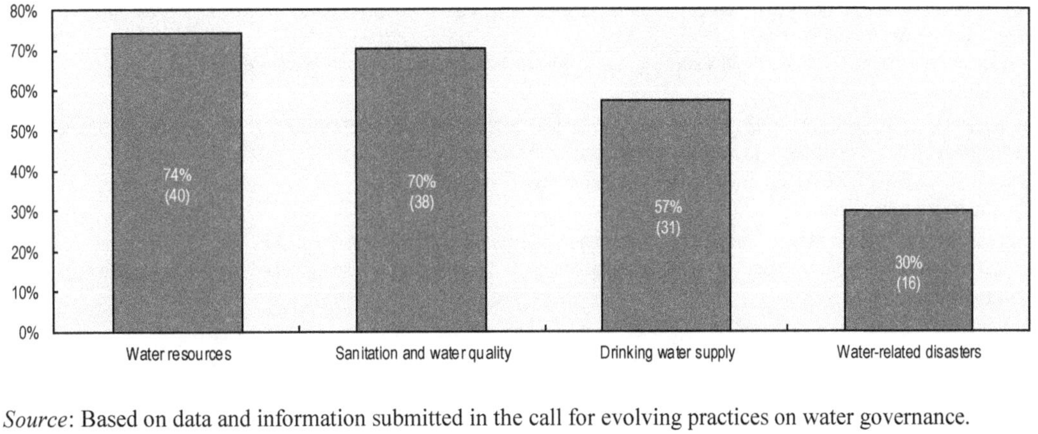

Source: Based on data and information submitted in the call for evolving practices on water governance.

All of the 12 *OECD Principles* on *Water Governance* are referenced in the 54 evolving practices, but to varying degrees. Principles 1, 3, 5, 8 and 10 are referenced in more than 65% of the practices; Principles 2, 4, 6, 9 and 12 are mentioned in 60% of the practices; and Principles 7 and 11 are only referred to in 52% of the practices (Figure 3.7).

Table 3.2. **Final set of evolving water governance practices by OECD Principle**

Principle 1: Clear roles and responsibilities

1. A water sector reform in Palestine (*Palestinian Water Authority*)
2. Adaptive governance to face fragmentation challenges in the Region of Alsace-Moselle (France) (*SDEA Alsace Moselle*)

Principle 2: Appropriate scales within basin systems

3. Evolving water governance frameworks in French water agencies (*Programme Solidarité-Eau*)
4. International co-operation and governance measures to fight micro-pollutants in the Rhine (*International Commission for the Protection of the Rhine*)
5. Evolving water governance to ensure drinking water supply in Vienna (Austria) (*Vienna Water – City of Vienna*)
6. Updating water governance in Brittany (France): From the regional level to the local level (*Conseil Régional de Bretagne*)
7. International river basin commissions of the Danube and Rhine – managing water at the right scale (*Austrian Federal Ministry of Agriculture, Forestry, Environment and Water Management*)
8. Implementing IWRM in Japanese river basins (*Japan Water Agency*)
9. Implementation of integrated water resources management approach in the Chikugo River Basin (Japan) (*Japan Water Agency*)
10. Alternative approach to river basin governance in Austria (*Austrian Federal Ministry of Agriculture, Forestry, Environment and Water Management*)
11. Governance tools to ensure conjunctive management of surface and groundwater in Australia (*Australian National University*)

Principle 3: Policy coherence

12. SANePLAN (Life Program of the European Commission): Ensuring policy coherence across sanitation services and urban planning (Spain and Italy) (*Fundación Instituto Tecnológico de Galicia*)

Principle 4: Capacity

13. Raising awareness and promoting education on drinking water in Austria (*Vienna Water – City of Vienna*)
14. Capacity-building in the drinking water supply sector by a professional organisation in Austria (*Association for Gas and Water, Austria*)
15. Implementing a water supply and sanitation programme in Burkina Faso (*GIZ*)
16. Promoting behavioural change in urban water consumption in Flanders (Belgium) (*Flanders Knowledge Center Water*)

Principle 5: Data and information

17. Open data to promote innovation in the water sector: Waves system (Netherlands) (*Dutch Water Authorities*)
18. Guiding decision making through better rural water services information systems in Kyrgyzstan (*United Nations Development Programme*)
19. Israel sewage information systems – an innovative water quality policy instrument (*Israeli Ministry of Environmental Protection*)
20. Improving data and information through institutional co-ordination in Turkey (*Turkish Ministry of Forestry and Water Affairs and Turkish Water Institute*)

Principle 6: Financing

21. Climate bonds: An innovative financial tool for the water sector (*Alliance for Global Water Adaptation*)
22. Water fund: A governance and financing mechanism for the Camboriu watershed (Brazil) (*The Nature Conservancy*)
23. Implementation of payment for ecosystem services scheme in the Pipiripau watershed (Brazil) (*Agência Reguladora da Águas, Energia e Saneamento Básico do Distrito Federal*)
24. Unlocking water investments in Zambia by implementing a solid governance framework (*Global Water Partnership*)

Principle 7: Regulatory frameworks

25. The rule of law and public participation in environmental flow regulations in Panama (*Environmental Advocacy Center of Panama*)
26. Implementing wastewater reuse policies in Israel (*Israeli Ministry of Environmental Protection*)
27. Indicators to monitor the enforcement of water regulatory frameworks in Kenya (*GIZ*)

Principle 8: Innovative governance

28. Framework conditions to favour the water-energy nexus in Vienna (*ebswien hauptkläranlage Ges.m.b.H.*)
29. From a local solution to a national strategy: Governance of environmental flows in the Copalita-Zimatán-Huatulco Basin (Mexico) (*WWF México*)

Principle 9: Integrity and transparency

30. Improving integrity in a river basin organisation in Indonesia (*Jasa TirtalPublic Corporation*)
31. The Danube River Basin Management Plan – an international accountability tool (*International Commission for the Protection of the Danube River*)

Principle 10: Stakeholder engagement

32. Effective stakeholder engagement for flood protection in the city of Pilsen (Czech Republic) (*Institute for Economic and Environmental Policy*)
33. Recovering ecosystems through stakeholder engagement: The case study of Lake Sihwa (Korea) (*K-water Institute*)
34. Sharing responsibilities with the civil society for protection against water-related disasters: Flood Brigade of Kampen (Netherlands) (*Dutch Water Authorities*)
35. Stakeholder engagement to restore ecosystems: The case of Lake Constance (Germany) (*Regional Council Tübingen*)
36. Misalignment of interests across stakeholder groups: The case of Rijnenburg (Netherlands) (*Utrecht University*)
37. Public advisory councils to promote access to safe drinking water supply in Tajikistan (*United Nations Development Programme*)
38. Stakeholder engagement to improve the delivery of water services in Karachi (Pakistan) (*Global Water Partnership*)

Table 3.2. **Final set of evolving water governance practices by OECD Principle** (*continued*)

Principle 11: Trade-offs between users, rural and urban areas, and generations	
39. Participatory diagnosis of access to water and sanitation services of vulnerable stakeholder groups: The case of Lima (Peru) (*Engineering Sciences and Global Development Research Group, Universitat Politècnica de Catalunya*)	
40. Assessing access to water and sanitation services of vulnerable stakeholder groups: The case of Castellón (Spain) (*Engineering Sciences and Global Development Research Group, Universitat Politècnica de Catalunya*)	
41. Using the OECD Principles to engage under-represented stakeholder groups in water governance: Fitzroy River Declaration (*Madjulla Inc*)	
42. Regulating and monitoring communal water services in southern Chad (*Initiative Développement*)	
Principle 12: Monitoring and evaluation	
43. Evaluating and monitoring governance in catchment-based institutions in Tanzania (*GIZ*)	
Cross-cutting evolving practices	
OECD Principle	**Name of the practice (*institution*)**
Principle 1: Clear roles and responsibilities Principle 10: Stakeholder engagement	44. Updating Ukraine's water governance system: From infrastructure to governance-oriented institutions (*Global Water Partnership-Ukraine, GWP-Ukraine*)
Principle 1: Clear roles and responsibilities Principle 8: Innovative governance	45. Co-ordinating an environmental recovery plan in the Segura river (Spain) (*Segura River Basin Authority*)
Principle 3: Policy coherence Principle 10: Stakeholder engagement	46. Increasing climate resiliency through stakeholder engagement in the Netherlands (*Dutch Water Authority De Dommel*)
Principle 6: Financing Principle 10: Stakeholder engagement	47. Sustainable solutions for climate-resilient cities through public-private partnerships (Alicante, Spain) (*AQUAE Chair in Water Economics*) 48. Overcoming conflict in a wastewater project in Jordan through stakeholder engagement (*SUEZ*)
Principle 1: Clear roles and responsibilities Principle 3: Policy coherence Principle 4: Capacity Principle 5: Data and information Principle 12: Monitoring and evaluation	49. Reform of the national water governance system in Ireland (*Irish Environmental Protection Agency*)
Principle 5: Data and information Principle 6: Financing	50. Willingness-to-pay for urban water services in Spanish municipalities (*ACCIONA Agua*)
Principle 6: Financing Principle 7: Regulatory frameworks Principle 12: Monitoring and evaluation	51. Implementation of a public policy for water services: The case of Portugal (*ERSAR Portugal*)
Principle 4: Capacity Principle 8: Innovative governance	52. A governance framework to implement alternative water supply solutions in the Mediterranean region (*Global Water Partnership*)
Principle 4: Capacity Principle 10: Stakeholder engagement	53. Improving water services delivery through stakeholder engagement in Jordan (*GIZ*)
Principle 6: Financing Principle 8: Innovative governance	54. Innovative water governance and local behaviour change in Payments for ecosystem services schemes in Colombia (*Rare*)

Note: The profiles of the 54 evolving practices will be available on line via a dedicated OECD website (forthcoming).

The 54 water evolving practices cover the five continents (America, Africa, Asia, Europe, Oceania) with more than half (52%) of the practices from the European Union. Asia (12%), Africa (9%), the Middle East (9%) and South America (7%) are also fairly-well represented with a lower representation for Eastern Europe and Oceania (4% each) and Central America (3%) (Figure 3.8). No practices were submitted for North America. OECD member countries and key partner countries are better represented than non-OECD economies, with 68% of practices from OECD member countries (32 practices), 7% from OECD key partner countries (namely, 4 practices from Brazil, Colombia and Peru), and 25% from non-OECD economies (14 practices).

Nine different types of stakeholder groups provided evolving practices. Governments (local, regional, national) and science and academia were the top contributors (22% and 17% respectively), followed by international organisations and service providers (13% each), watershed institutions and civil society (11% each), donors (7%), and regulators (4%). One evolving practice was submitted by an indigenous community from Australia (Practice No. 4) (Figure 3.9).

Figure 3.7. **Share of evolving practices referencing each of the OECD Principles**

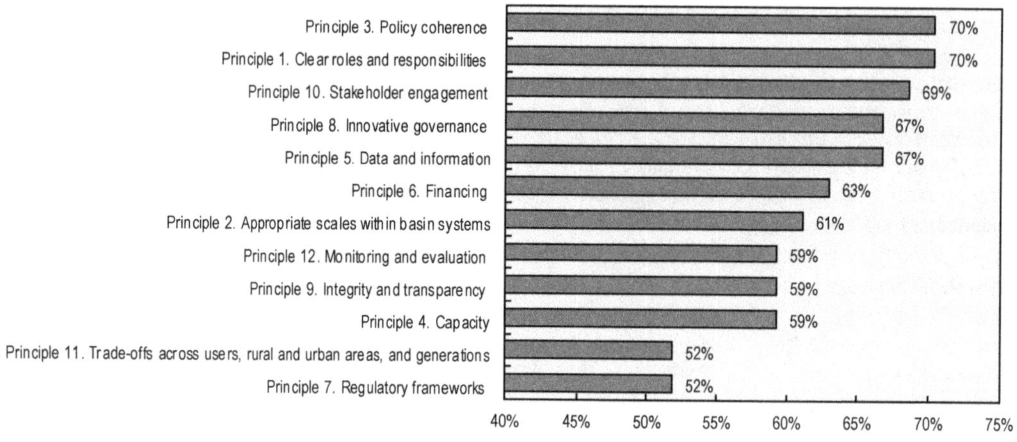

Source: Based on the data and information submitted in the evolving practices on water governance.

Figure 3.8. **Evolving practices by geographical region**

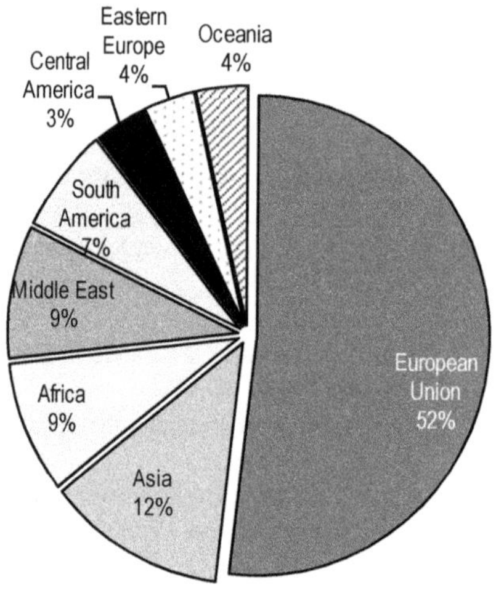

Source: Based on data and information submitted in the call for evolving practices on water governance.

All relevant scales of water governance (from local to international) are represented throughout the practices. The majority of examples demonstrate practices at either the local (24 practices) and national level (22 practices) (Figure 3.10), with some practices that cut across two or more scales, e.g. national and basin scale. Some examples of cross-cutting practices include: 1) Practice No. 3, which shows the governance transformations experienced by French water agencies; 2) Practice No. 10 from Austria, which provides an alternative approach to river basin governance concerning the national, basin and regional levels.

Figure 3.9. **Share of evolving practices provided by typology of stakeholders**

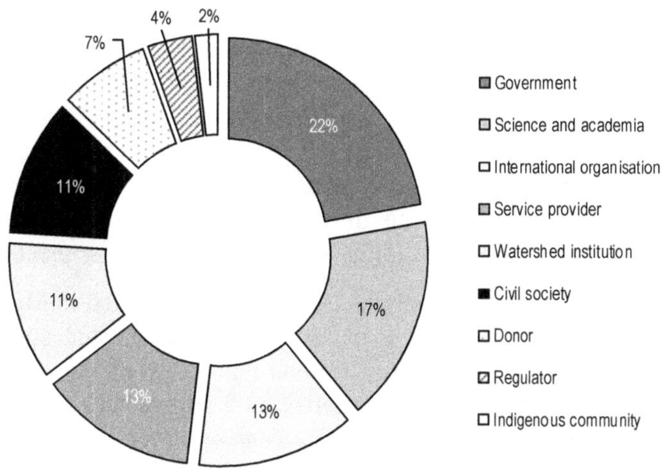

Source: Based on data and information submitted in the call for evolving practices on water governance.

The practices collected range across time frames, including some examples that are less than one year old (39%) and others that have been in place for more ten years (11%) (Figure 3.11). The remaining practices span different time periods: 5-10 years (15%), 3-5 years (18%) and 1-3 years (17%). Water governance reforms or processes are easier to evaluate the longer they are running, which likely explains why the set of evolving practices collected has a greater number of examples that have been active for more than ten years. At the time of writing, 39 out of the 54 practices of the final set are still ongoing.

Figure 3.10. **Evolving practices by scale**

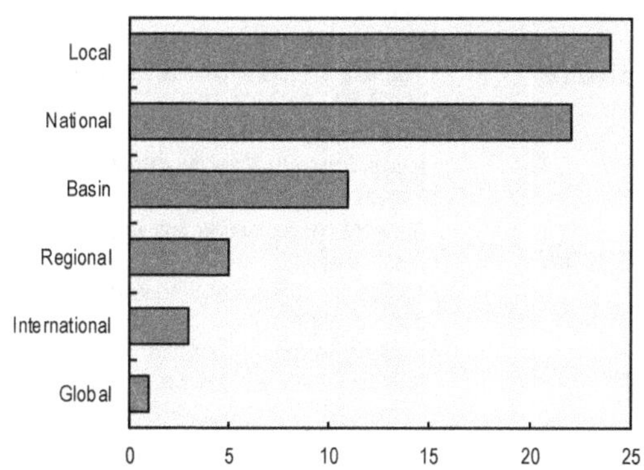

Source: Based on data and information submitted in the call for evolving practices on water governance.

Figure 3.11. **Evolving practices by time frame**

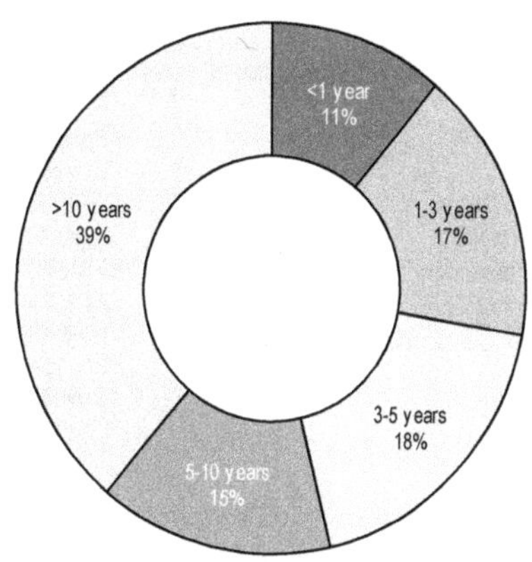

Source: Based on data and information submitted in the call for evolving practices on water governance.

Methodology to develop a set of evolving practices

The process to develop the set of evolving water governance practices consisted of three main steps, namely: 1) collection of evolving practices; 2) selection of evolving practices.

Collection

A three-part template was developed to collect information on evolving practices. The aim was to harmonise the presentation of case studies and to enhance their readability. The template requires respondents to complete three distinct sections: 1) profile of the practice with key descriptions (who, what, when, why and where); 2) linking the practice to the *OECD Principles on Water Governance*; 3) assessment of the practice in terms of costs and benefits, progress and replicability potential. Together, these parts are meant to highlight key features, provide evidence of implementation, include feedback (costs, benefits, impact) and illustrate the replicability potential of the cases selected.

A call to collect evolving water governance practices was issued in March 2017 using an online version of the template shown in Figure 3.12. Interested stakeholders were encouraged to submit practices that covered a broad range of topics or countries with the following criteria: 1) relate to any of the water-related sub-sectors (services, resources, flood, environment, etc.); 2) target any scale of governance (local, basin, regional, national or global); 3) concern any category of stakeholders (government, citizens, service providers, regulators, etc.); and 4) be from an OECD country or non-OECD economy.

Figure 3.12. **Template to collect evolving practices**

Block 1: Profile of the practice (who, what, when, why and where)	Block 2: Linking the practice to the OECD Principles	Block 3: Assessment of the practice in terms of costs and benefits, progress and replicability potential
• Contact point • Title • Five key words • Brief general description • Hyperlinks to additional online information on the practice • Location of the practice (i.e. country, region, city) • Scale of the practice (national, basin, local, other) • Socio-economic context of the practice • Key milestones • Time frame • Key stakeholders involved • Water function(s) • Related Sustainable Development Goals	• Principle 1: Clear roles and responsibilities • Principle 2: Appropriate scales within basin systems • Principle 3: Policy coherence • Principle 4: Capacity • Principle 5: Data and information • Principle 6: Financing • Principle 7: Regulatory frameworks • Principle 8: Innovative governance • Principle 9: Integrity and transparency • Principle 10: Stakeholder engagement • Principle 11: Trade-offs across users, rural and urban areas, and generations • Principle 12: Monitoring and evaluation	• Mechanism to estimate costs incurred • Monetary and non-monetary costs incurred by the practice (i.e. financial/ human resources, capacities required, etc.)? • Implementation challenges and ways forward • Mechanism to monitor progress • Indicators to review your practice over time • Tangible progress achieved • Mechanism to evaluate the impacts • Impacts achieved/expected • Achievement sustainable and why • Lessons learnt • Applicability/transferability to other contexts or places • Enabling framework conditions to replicate/transfer the practice

Practices were collected by the OECD Water Governance Initiative through activities carried out by its members, such as policy dialogues, consultations, in-depth studies, as well as "scans" related to water governance in their programmes of work. The WGI members also played a critical role in disseminating the call for contributions among their networks and constituencies. An initial set of 69 practices was collected between April and May 2017.

Screening

Practices submitted for consideration had to adhere to a minimum set of criteria presented in the template (Figure 3.13). Submissions could also be ongoing "narratives" of collective learning. The practices submitted were reviewed to ensure that the minimum criteria were met. Reviewers also scanned submissions for examples with strong potential for replicability and relevance to water governance. Sixty-nine evolving practices were collected and reviewed, including 30 practices that were deemed ready for peer-learning, 35 that needed additional information, and 4 that were considered not applicable. A final set of 54 evolving practices was selected for peer-to-peer dialogue.

Figure 3.13. **Minimum criteria for screening of evolving practices**

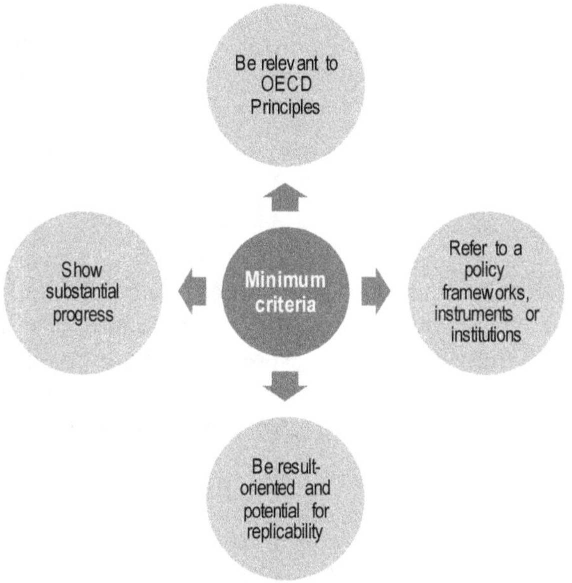

A qualitative analysis of the evolving practices

A qualitative analysis was conducted to investigate the policy frameworks, institutions and instruments of each of the practices, and how they helped to achieve policy objectives. The analysis highlights common points, cross-cutting messages and lessons learnt on water governance. It is important to note that the practices are neither peer reviewed nor fact-checked. The work on evolving practices is voluntary and although a qualitative analysis of the practices collected has helped draw lessons to improve water governance, the ultimate objective is to promote peer learning among different actors. In particular, the caveats of this exercise include:

- Evolving practices were taken at "face value". Any bias linked to the practice providers or errors in the original data or text of the case study were not reviewed. The analysis did not go beyond the information already provided in the templates.
- Interpretation errors of the practices descriptions. Some sections of the templates might have been interpreted differently from the original purpose of the practice provider.
- Practices vary from individual projects such as waste treatment works in a given city to national, systemic reform of water governance covering multiple sectors and regions. Lessons learnt should therefore be taken with caution due to the variety of situations and contexts.
- The analysis provides a high-level overview, which may not include the level of detail required to understand individual case studies.

- The assessment of the OECD Principles was especially difficult to determine from the information provided. The practices are retrospective evaluations by providers that sometimes tended to demonstrate adherence to as many Principles as possible. Furthermore, many of the cases submitted were not advanced enough to fully demonstrate the Principles in use.
- Terminology and language cannot be assumed to be homogenous in the case studies. For instance, "policy" could mean many different things across the practices.
- Rather than assess each practice separately against a set of factors, the exercise sought to build a narrative by drawing examples from selected practices and looking for commonalities and patterns.

Impact of governance on water outcomes

Despite the diversity of contexts analysed in the evolving practices, three types of impacts emerged: 1) better provision of water services; 2) improvements in the environment, ecology and biodiversity; 3) risk reduction of water-related disaster. This does not imply that there are no other type of impacts, such as cost reduction or more efficient land-use practices, but rather that these three groups were the most observed in the analysis. It also does not mean that there is a one-to-one correlation between the practices and the impacts; in some cases, the practice contributed to one, two or all of the impacts.

Water services

The impact of practices in improving water services delivery is noticeable in drinking water supply and wastewater treatment. Better water governance, either through enforcing new regulation, participatory approaches, policy coherence or innovative governance, has translated into better quality water services in a number of cases. The practices where this impact is more clearly identifiable and measurable are those that followed a long-term approach to securing access to clean water services. For instance, the strategy followed by the city of Vienna since the 1850s to protect its freshwater sources has resulted in both investments in hard infrastructure and measures to strengthen the water services governance system (Practice No. 5). In the 1870s, the city constructed a major channel that virtually eliminated all waterborne diseases due to the supply of better quality water. Today, the city of Vienna and its public service provider (Vienna Water) measure impact through external evaluations and customer satisfaction surveys and in both the results are excellent for the city. Vienna has been ranked eight times by the Mercer survey as the city with the highest quality of living worldwide, explicitly mentioning water supply as a key factor. Another good example is the public policy for water services implemented in Portugal from 1993 to 2016 (Practice No. 51). This national policy has allowed Portugal to become one of the top performers in the EU in terms of drinking water quality standards (99% of water supplied complies with EU standards) and households served by public water systems increased from 81% to 96%. The same is observed for public sewerage systems, where there has been an increase from 60% to 82% of households have decreased from hundreds cases per year to nearly zero.

Contribution of governance to environment, ecology and biodiversity

The benefits of good governance for the wider environment, ecology and biodiversity were a focus in a large number of practices. The impacts ranged in terms of type, with some related to recovering watershed ecosystems or reducing pollution in a certain water source (e.g. river and lake), as well as scale for water management, i.e. local, basin, national and international.

- At the local level, the artificial lake located in the Sihwa District (Korea) exemplifies how the collective efforts of the central government, local authorities, private sector, local residents and experts resulted in a great improvement of the quality of water (Practice No. 33). After the construction of Lake Sihwa in 1994, the quality of the water deteriorated to levels of 17.4 parts per million (ppm) of chemical oxygen demand (COD) in 1997. Among others, poor water management and illegal actions, such as garbage dumping, illegal alteration of land shape and illegal construction and occupation, were the main reasons for this alteration in the quality. In 2004, the government established the Sihwa District Sustainable Development Council, a consultative body with representatives of all the above-mentioned sectors. Their efforts have resulted in an increase of the wildlife living in the lake area and a reduction from the 17.4 ppm to 3.7 ppm of COD in 2008.
- At basin level, two practices in Brazil reported how establishing a payment for ecosystem services contributed to the improvement of ecosystem services. The "Camboriu payments for watershed service" was created in 2013 to remediate the large water losses for municipal water supply and the high sediment loading, which were being experienced in the watershed (Practice No. 22). Outcomes expected by 2030 include the conservation of around 3 900 ha conserved/protected and the restoration of 300 ha, which will improve the quality of the water in the watershed and consequently the municipal water supply. In the Pipiripau watershed (Brazil) (Practice No. 23), a diagnostic in 2010 revealed that of the 424 properties in the basin 84% of users were not complying with land protection regulations, which was having an impact on the quality of available water resources in the basin. The Water Producer Program, an initiative of 18 institutional partners (public, private, non-governmental organisations [NGOs] and research centres), involved over 137 farms in the programme that are raising funds to implement conservation measures in over 886 ha and restoration measures in 305 ha. The expected impact is a reduction of 40% of the original erosion and sedimentation and an increase of 5-10% of the base flow in the basin.
- At national level, Portugal achieved a relevant impact in water services (Practice No. 51), reporting an increase from 58% to 98% and from 17% to 90% of good quality water for bathing in coastal waters and rivers, respectively. Moreover, waterborne diseases moved from hundreds of cases per year to close to zero. Indeed, the country has reaped the benefits of improvements in access to drainage and wastewater treatment. Households with access to public sewerage systems increased from 60% to 83%, and 82% of those households are connected to a wastewater treatment plant. The majority of the remaining situations are solved through individual solutions such as septic tanks.
- At international level, the International Commission for the Protection of the Rhine, formed by the European Commission, Austria, the Belgian region of Wallonia, France, Germany, Italy, Liechtenstein, Luxemburg, the Netherlands and Switzerland, designed a strategy in 2013 to prevent micro-pollutants effluents from urban wastewater and diffuse sources reaching the Rhine and its tributaries (Practice No. 4). A variety of measures were featured in the strategy, including improving the information systems tracking the effluents, expanding the

knowledge base on eco-toxicological reactions in the basin, and implementing a range of water treatment approaches. Overall, the International Commission for the Protection of the Rhine's work has improved the environmental status of the Rhine by reducing contamination at large and recovering the ecosystems in the basin. The strategy on micro-pollutants is still ongoing.

Governance contribution to addressing water-related disasters

The evolving practices also report impacts in terms of reducing water-related risks, namely floods and droughts.

- **Risks of too little water.** In the Mediterranean region, the Global Water Partnership launched a Non-Conventional Water Resources (NCWR) Programme to increase water availability in water scarce islands. The practice presents alternative water supply solutions used in islands in Cyprus,[1] Greece, Italy and Malta, and the governance frameworks that make these solutions succeed (Practice No. 52). The programme focused on alternative small-scale rainwater harvesting and greywater recycling applications. Infrastructure measures were coupled with educational, capacity-building and awareness-raising activities. The programme also promoted the upscale of local practices with the objective of incorporating them into local, subnational and national strategies. A tangible impact was seen in Malta, where the National Water Management Plan included NCWR solutions as part of the water security strategy of the country. Another example was seen in Australia, where governance reforms to allow for improvements in conjunctive management of surface and groundwater leading to a reduction of risk of too little water (Practice No. 11). The recovery of water entitlements and reforms in the institutional setting led to water storage both in aquifers and surface reservoirs. The impact of such measures has been particularly noticeable in the dry states of South Australia and Western Australia and in the cities of Perth and Adelaide. The conjunctive management measures have been coupled with NCWR solutions. The city of Perth has set a target for recycling 30% of all metropolitan wastewater by 2030, and South Australia has set targets of recycling 60 gigalitres of stormwater and 75 gigalitres of wastewater for non-human use by 2050.
- **Risks of too much water.** In Alicante (Spain), a public-private partnership invested in a multi-purpose park (called "La Marjal") that would control floods, reuse water, provide an ecosystem for local species and serve for recreational uses (Practice No. 47). The park prevented flooding in the touristic area of San Juan beach after a historic flood episode on 16 March 2017, which registered a rain of 140 litres/m² in two hours (the third-largest rainfall recorded since 1934). The park has reduced risks of urban floods and made the city of Alicante more resilient to climate change. Similarly, in the city of Pilsen (Czech Republic), the local government undertook the implementation of small-scale nature-based measures in urban areas to adapt to the increasing risk of floods due to climate change (the costs of the 2002 flood in the city of Pilsen were estimated around EUR 20.8 million) (Practice No. 32). These nature-based measures are mostly on private land; therefore, a strong outreach campaign to engage stakeholders was needed to showcase the benefits of the measures (based on a cost-benefit analysis conducted by the Institute for Economic and Environmental Policy). The success of this intervention led to the development of an adaptation strategy for the city of Pilsen that puts ecosystem-based approaches at the core to reduce flood risks.

Prominent governance enablers

The qualitative analysis of evolving practices identified several factors that can enable transformation (herein understood as improvement in the situation as identified by the practice description) in water governance. These factors included clear identification and understanding of challenges faced and possible solutions to cope with them; adequacy of institutional frameworks, human and technical capacities and skills; strong leadership of certain actors (e.g. political will of a ministry); willingness to co-operate, support and manage trade-offs; stakeholder engagement to share responsibilities in the implementation of water policies; sufficient and stable finance; accurate data and information; and enough time to experience the improvements. Since governance contexts are different, not all the mentioned enablers are equally important to achieve transformation in a specific context. The following sections provide some examples related to three cross-cutting enablers that are present in the majority of practices and were helpful to achieving policy objectives, namely: effective stakeholder engagement, sufficient and stable financing, and strong political will.

Effective stakeholder engagement

Stakeholder engagement is mentioned in nearly every water governance practice in the final set. In particular, early engagement of stakeholders was acknowledged as a key for success, creating acceptability and ownership of policy reform processes, strategy design (e.g. adaptation to climate change, etc.) or project implementation (e.g. construction of a new wastewater plant, etc.). Raising awareness among civil society on water governance and environmental issues, as well as capacity building of actors involved in engagement processes, were also highlighted throughout a wide number of practices. In the practices reviewed, engagement happened between the government and other actors (users, private sector, NGOs, universities, etc.), between different communities (e.g. upstream and downstream users or urban areas and rural settlements), and between water service providers and users (customers or water users at large). Below are some examples of the stakeholder engagement processes that contributed to the achievement of wider policy or project objectives.

- Policy design. In Ukraine, water governance reform was handed over from the Agency for Water Infrastructure (Vodkhoz) (inherited from the Soviet Union) with a mandate focused on infrastructure development, to a Water Resources Agency with a wider mandate (Practice No. 44). In 2016, Global Water Partnership Ukraine (GWP Ukraine) launched a national policy dialogue, "Rethinking of Water Security for Ukraine", to undertake stakeholder consultations to support the water governance reform. The dialogue aimed to reach consensus on the strategic vision, long-term goals and objectives of Ukraine's water policy. One of the results of this dialogue was input to the country's 2030 Water Strategy and the implementation roadmap of SDG 6 at national level. Moreover, the GWP has been accepted as a neutral platform for dialogues around water issues. In Ireland, a new National Water Forum was established to facilitate better engagement with a wide range of actors at national level. The forum provided independent analysis and commentary on the draft National River Basin Plan for the 2nd cycle of the Water Framework Directive (Practice No. 49).
- Project design. In Alicante (Spain), involving stakeholders early in the project led to choosing a green infrastructure option (a flooding park) rather than other more traditional solutions to solve the flooding problems of a touristic area of the city

(Practice No. 47). The parties that participated in the decision-making process included the public sector, private operators, civil society organisations, environmental NGOs and the public at large. The same stakeholders helped decide which flora and fauna were more appropriate to introduce in the new ecosystem created by the park.

In Lake Constance (Germany), the lack of public engagement associated with the implementation of a renaturation strategy led to a litigation process (Practice No. 35). Lake Constance and its shoreline have an undeniable status for the region: environmental value that was a trigger for the development of human settlements in the area and the economic development of local companies tightly linked to heavy touristic activity. The city of Kressbronn (located near the lake) sought to restore habitats and further develop the city. To this end, the city, in co-operation with the state government, developed a series of renaturation plans, which were criticized by local residents and resulted in lawsuit by affected residents against the plans. After a long trial (2002-15), the court ruled in support of the renaturation plans, but the Regional Council of Tübingen recognised the need for public buy-in and in 2016 put in a place a process to include citizens, local businesses and civil society organisations in discussions about the plans and the possibility for future amendments.

Sufficient and stable financing

Many practices mentioned sufficient and stable financing as an important success factor. In Jordan and Israel, the financial viability of a wastewater plant over its lifetime and the wastewater system as a whole depended on appropriate tariff levels to secure cost recovery and future investments (Practices No. 48 and 26, respectively). In Austria, securing public investment in water services was key to achieving the full implementation of the EU Urban Waste Water Treatment Directive in 2005. Investments in wastewater treatment started in 1959, with a focus on restoring the good ecological status of lakes, and shifted towards urban and rural areas in the 1990s. Since 1959, Austria has invested about EUR 46.3 billion to support drinking water supply and wastewater treatment infrastructure. Currently, around EUR 500 million are invested per year in water infrastructure, and investments focus mainly in maintaining and restoring existing infrastructure to ensure water services levels (Practice No. 10).

Strong political will

Lastly, political will to improve water governance as a means to achieve policy objectives is an overarching factor that enables effective co-ordination, stakeholder engagement, and sufficient and stable finance. Reforms of legislative frameworks are often an indicator of political will, whether at national (federal or state) level or to implement supranational legislation such as the EU Water Framework Directive. In Karachi (Pakistan), a territorial reform that led to a reduction in the competences of municipalities turned into an enabling factor to improve drinking water supply and sanitation provision, whereby community activity and engagement became even more important (Practice No. 38). In the Segura River Basin, the poor quality of the water led the regional government to pass a new piece of legislation to improve wastewater management. This law included four main measures: 1) assigning wastewater management competences to the Regional Department for Agriculture and Water; 2) designing and implementing a "Master Plan for Urban and Wastewater Treatment in the Murcia Region 2001-2010"; 3) implementing a levy for wastewater effluents; 4) creating a public company responsible for operating and maintaining wastewater infrastructures. All these measures make up the Segura River Project, led by the Regional Water Directorate, with the active involvement of the Segura River Basin Authority, city councils in the region and the European Union (Practice No. 45).

Examples of evolving practices showcasing the OECD Principles

The evolving practices show practical experiences of countries at various levels (local, basin, national) that could help identify ways forward for the implementation of the *OECD Principles on Water Governance*. In particular, these practical experiences encompass the "what", "who", and "how". The "what" captures the policy and legal frameworks that represent the basis for the allocation of roles and responsibilities, the development of water policies and the implementation of water governance instruments; the "who" identifies formal institutions in charge of defining, implementing and evaluating water policies, as well as developing projects and programmes and producing and collecting data, etc.; and the "how" reports on the instruments through which water policies are implemented and evaluated. The next sections cluster those lessons around the *OECD Principles on Water Governance* (see Chapter 1).

Principle 1: Clear roles and responsibilities

Clearly allocate and distinguish roles and responsibilities for water policy making, policy implementation, operational management and regulation, and foster co-ordination across these responsible authorities. To that effect, legal and institutional frameworks should:

- Specify the allocation of roles and responsibilities across all levels of government and water-related institutions in regard to water:
  - policy making, especially priority setting and strategic planning
  - policy implementation especially financing and budgeting, data and information, stakeholder engagement, capacity development and evaluation
  - operational management, especially service delivery, infrastructure operation and investment
  - regulation and enforcement, especially tariff setting, standards, licensing, monitoring and supervision, control and audit, and conflict management.
- Help identify and address gaps, overlaps and conflicts of interest through effective co-ordination at and across all levels of government.

Evolving practices showcasing Principle 1:

- In the Segura River Project (Spain) clarifying roles and responsibilities was key to mobilise sufficient and stable finance for wastewater management. The law (§30) deconcentrated the competence for wastewater management from the national water authority to the regional Department for Agriculture and Water (within the government of the region of Murcia). The department was the lead institution for implementation of the plan and ensured that key water-related actors in the basin were actively involved, namely the Segura River Basin Authority and local governments, such as Murcia and other smaller municipalities. To date, the plan has cost EUR 645 million and has been financed through European Cohesion Policy funds (75-80% of the project's budget) and by the national, regional and local governments (Practice No. 45).

- In Ireland, a comprehensive review of the first Water Framework Directive (WFD) implementation cycle led in 2015 to a water governance reform. The target of the first cycle was to achieve a 14% improvement in water quality. However, the results showed a slight disimprovement overall. The Irish government concluded that the governance structures in terms of who does what, how and at which level of government were not clearly set and hindered the effective implementation of the WFD. The ongoing reform foresees three tiers of governments with very clear differentiated competences: Tier 1, the Department of Housing, Planning, Community and Local Government has the responsibility for water policy and legislation; Tier 2, the Environmental Protection Agency is in charge of science, evidence and reporting the findings; Tier 3, local authorities are in charge of local implementation and public engagement (Practice No. 49).
- In Palestine, the institutional fragility of the water sector was generally acknowledged in a number of reports. The institutional framework created in 1995 to manage water resources and services lacked a clear mandate. The latter impaired the development of adequate policies and strategies for water resources management, infrastructure development and service provision. Therefore, the Palestinian Authority endorsed an Action Plan for Reform with the objective of establishing strong sustainable institutions within legal frameworks that clearly define roles, responsibilities and the interface between them (Practice No. 1).

Principle 2: Appropriate scales within basin systems

Manage water at the appropriate scale(s) within integrated basin governance systems to reflect local conditions, and foster co-ordination between the different scales. To that effect, water management practices and tools should:

- respond to long-term environmental, economic and social objectives with a view to making the best use of water resources, through risk prevention and integrated water resources management
- encourage a sound hydrological cycle management from capture and distribution of freshwater to the release of wastewater and return flows
- promote adaptive and mitigation strategies, action programmes and measures based on clear and coherent mandates, through effective basin management plans that are consistent with national policies and local conditions
- promote multi-level co-operation among users, stakeholders and levels of government for the management of water resources
- enhance riparian co-operation on the use of transboundary freshwater resources.

Evolving practices showcasing Principle 2:

- Australia has recognised the concept of "water territories". These go beyond the limits set by basins to also take into account the integration between surface and groundwater as well as water transfers. Following the millennium drought (2002-09), the country established the Australian National Water Initiative, a joint commitment of the national and regional governments to make water use more efficient and sustainable. The National Water Initiative acknowledges the connectivity between surface and groundwater and calls for conjunct management of these systems. As such, the 2012 Murray Darling Basin Plan foresees not only boundaries based on surface water sources, but also takes into account groundwater use (Practice No. 11).

- To implement the Water Framework Directive, Austria, a small federal country (nine provinces) crossed by three large transboundary river basins, decided to follow an alternative approach to basin governance that does not foresee basin institutions. The country built on existing administrative federal structures to ensure co-ordination and co-operation at the basin level. River basin management plans and flood risk management plans play a key role in this context. The Austrian Water Act entitles the Federal Ministry as the lead institution to design and implement river basin management plans and flood risk management plans. The draft plans are then submitted to the provinces for comments, and finally they run through a public participation process. The different actions that feature in the programme of measures are assigned to the authority according to the scale of intervention (Practice No. 10).

Principle 3: Policy coherence

Encourage policy coherence through effective cross-sectoral co-ordination, especially between policies for water and the environment, health, energy, agriculture, industry, spatial planning and land use through:

- encouraging co-ordination mechanisms to facilitate coherent policies across ministries, public agencies and levels of government, including cross-sectoral plans
- fostering co-ordinated management of use, protection and clean-up of water resources, taking into account policies that affect water availability, quality and demand (e.g. agriculture, forestry, mining, energy, fisheries, transportation, recreation and navigation) as well as risk prevention
- identifying, assessing and addressing the barriers to policy coherence from practices, policies and regulations within and beyond the water sector, using monitoring, reporting and reviews
- providing incentives and regulations to mitigate conflicts among sectoral strategies, bringing these strategies into line with water management needs and finding solutions that fit with local governance and norms.

Evolving practices showcasing Principle 3:

- In the catchment area of the Dommel (Netherlands), a flooding event served as a wake-up call to understand that horizontal co-ordination across water-related sectors is essential to increase climate resilience. The heavy rains in June 2016, accompanied by hailstones of 10 cm of diameter, caused numerous damages in the south of the Netherlands (estimations say over EUR 500 million). Following this event, the regional water authority organised a multi-stakeholder dialogue to find solutions for the climate scenarios forecasted for 2050. One of the main outcomes of this dialogue was the acknowledgment of all parties to create a climate-resilient water system that would take all on board. The latter included a wide range of policy domains, including energy, urban development, ageing, health and transport (Practice No. 46).
- The project "SANePLAN" (Integrated Planning and Sustainable Management of Sanitation Infrastructures through Innovative Precision Technology, funded by the Life Program of European Commission), developed an online geographic

information system (GIS) focused on improving policy coherence between sanitation and land-use policies. The information system is open to the public and simulates different scenarios in terms of population growth, environmental protection regulation or climate change, among others. Foundation Technological Institute of Galicia (research institute), in collaboration with the province of Pontevedra (Spain) and the Italian company Physis S.r.l. (Italian company), developed the pilot system, which was tested in five municipalities (with more than 45 000 inhabitants) located in Italy and Spain (Practice No. 12).

- Co-ordinating committees are a tool in Ireland to ensure policy coherence across national authorities responsible for water and other environmental and agricultural policies. In 2014, national water governance reform established a Water Policy Advisory Committee chaired by the Department of Housing, Planning, Community and Local Government. This platform provides a policy framework to co-ordinate the implementation of WFD, the Floods Directive and Marine Framework Directive and other key water-related directives (Urban Waste Water Directive, Bathing Water Directive, Shellfish Directive, Drinking Water Directive) and associated environmental European directives (Habitats Directive). The Department of Agriculture, Food and the Marine participates actively in the committee to ensure cross-sectoral co-ordination between water issues and the Rural Development Programme (Practice No. 49).

Principle 4: Capacity

Adapt the level of capacity of responsible authorities to the complexity of water challenges to be met, and to the set of competencies required to carry out their duties, through:

- identifying and addressing capacity gaps to implement integrated water resources management, notably for planning, rule-making, project management, finance, budgeting, data collection and monitoring, risk management and evaluation
- matching the level of technical, financial and institutional capacity in water governance systems to the nature of problems and needs
- encouraging adaptive and evolving assignment of competences upon demonstration of capacity, where appropriate
- promoting the hiring of public officials and water professionals that uses merit-based, transparent processes that are independent from political cycles
- promoting education and training of water professionals to strengthen the capacity of water institutions as well as stakeholders at large and to foster co-operation and knowledge-sharing.

Evolving practices showcasing Principle 4:

- In Austria, professional associations promote the education and training of water professionals to strengthen the capacity of water institutions as well as stakeholders at large. The Austrian Association for Water & Gas (OVGW) is a pioneer and key actor in the professional training sector in Austria. In 1970, the OVGW launched the first seminars and the Masters for drinking water operators, which were the first programmes in Austria dedicated to training drinking water utility personnel. In 2000, the Water Masters received the EN ISO 17024 accreditation from the Ministry of Economics, and in 2002, the Ministry of Health certified that the OVGW's training programmes comply with the requirements set in the Drinking Water Act for personnel to work in public utilities (Practice No. 14).
- In Ireland, one of the challenges identified was the lack of capacity for policy implementation at local level. The strict embargo of staff replacement and hiring between 2008 and 2014 led to a loss of water staff and expertise at all levels of government. Consequently, local authorities had too much responsibility without the necessary authority and monetary resources. In 2014, public sector hiring recommenced, albeit at very controlled levels, and both the Environmental Protection Agency and local authorities received additional and targeted resources. In addition, the creation of a small but highly skilled Catchment Management and Science Unit strengthened the knowledge base for river basin management. Since 2014, this unit has carried out the bulk of the science and evidence work that underpins the draft National River Basin Management Plan. Another measure created the Local Authority Water and Community Office, comprised of 12 community water officers and responsible for improving stakeholder engagement at regional and local level (Practice No. 49).
- In Jordan, the Ministry of Water and Irrigation realised the importance of building capacity on water resources management. With the support of GIZ, the Ministry created a committee for engaging local and national actors, including representatives of the local communities, Syrian refugees, the Ministry, the Water Authority of Jordan, Yarmouk Water Company, municipalities, mosques, schools, NGOs and other relevant actors. One of the key objectives of this initiative is to identify and train stakeholders on several topics related to water management, including community development, participatory decision making or conflict management skills, amongst others (Practice No. 53).
- In Flanders, Belgium improving the capacity to conduct water scans of local administrations was one of the key elements of the "rational water use in buildings as a stepping stone towards water wise cities" project that aims to achieve a 30% reduction of water consumption. The project is driving a structural reform to adapt the competence profiles of technicians to the capacity gaps identified in the local administration. For this purpose, starting in September 2018, educational centres will offer more tailored training to professionals in the sector. The objective is to have professionals with the right knowledge and expertise to analyse water consumption, inform the user about water-saving measures, and carry out the necessary installation and maintenance works (Practice No. 16).

Principle 5: Data and information

Produce, update and share timely, consistent, comparable, and policy-relevant water and water-related data and information, and use it to guide, assess and improve water policy, through:

- defining requirements for cost-effective and sustainable production and methods for sharing high-quality water and water-related data and information, e.g. on the status of water resources, water financing, environmental needs, socio-economic features and institutional mapping
- fostering effective co-ordination and experience-sharing among organisations and agencies producing water-related data between data producers and users, and across levels of government
- promoting engagement with stakeholders in the design and implementation of water information systems, and providing guidance on how such information should be shared to foster transparency, trust and comparability (e.g. data banks, reports, maps, diagrams, observatories)
- encouraging the design of harmonised and consistent information systems at the basin scale, including in the case of transboundary water, to foster mutual confidence, reciprocity and comparability within the framework of agreements between riparian countries
- reviewing data collection, use, sharing and dissemination to identify overlaps and synergies and track unnecessary data overload.

Evolving practices showcasing Principle 5:

- In Kyrgyzstan, improving data collection for rural water services has informed policy discussions and guided budgeting decisions from national sources and international development partners. In 2016, the National Statistic Committee, in collaboration with relevant ministries for water policies in Kyrgyzstan and the UNDP GoAL WaSH, developed and implemented a water services reporting form for rural areas that will be used on an annual basis. The form produces timely, comparable and coherent data. It has helped to adjust the Action Plan of the National Strategy of Drinking Water Supply and Sanitation. Based on the data reported for 2016, and the needs revealed, the national budget for rural drinking water supply increased from approximately USD 1.17 million in 2016 to USD 3.0 million in 2017. At the same time, thanks to the reliable information provided, support from development partners will increase up to USD 70.0 million until 2023 (Practice No. 18).
- In Israel, a new tariff established for industries producing effluents with a high concentration of pollutants has encouraged the development of a high-tech information system for water quality. The environmental regulations that control the effluents produced by the industries exist since the 1980s and 1990s. However, it was not until the tariff was set in 2011 that the technologies used for monitoring those effluents improved significantly. The new online measuring systems provide useful information that guides water services management, such as forecast changes in water consumption, quasi-real time leakage detection, etc. As a result, municipal water and sewage corporations have improved the quality of the water services delivered (water leakages have decreased from approximately 30% ten years ago to a national average of less than 11%) (Practice No. 19).

- In 2013, Turkey started a project to create an online National Water Information System (NWIS) that compiles nationwide data on water quality and quantity, allocation regimes and water-related risks. The ultimate objective of the project is to transform Turkey's approach to water governance, moving from silo logic to more integrated practices. The NWIS will be the first initiative in Turkey to break through institutional silos and show water data at basin level. The project also aims to encourage all water-related public, private and civil actors to be active stakeholders in data production. Furthermore, the NWIS will help identify data gaps and duplications, thus improving water governance efficiency by making better use of the existing time and resources. The NWIS will gather data, maps, statistics and policy documents under nine modules: environmental infrastructure, basin management, climate change, groundwater, surface water, water quality, drought, floods and water allocation (Practice No. 20).
- In Ireland, improvement in water data and information is a fundamental building block for investment decisions. Ireland has followed a tiered approach to characterisation, which has resulted in structured data and scientific evidence at national, catchment (46), sub-catchment (583) and water body (4 000) levels. The data are all gathered into one new IT application called the WFD Application, operated by the Irish Environmental Protection Agency, and all public bodies involved in water management and protection in Ireland have access to it (Practice No. 49).

Principle 6: Financing

Ensure that governance arrangements help mobilise water finance and allocate financial resources in an efficient, transparent and timely manner, through:

- promoting governance arrangements that help water institutions across levels of government raise the necessary revenues to meet their mandates, building through for example principles such as the polluter-pays and user-pays, as well as payment for environmental services
- carrying out sector reviews and strategic financial planning to assess short-, medium-, and long-term investment and operational needs and take measures to help ensure the availability and sustainability of such finance
- adopting sound and transparent practices for budgeting and accounting that provide a clear picture of water activities and any associated contingent liabilities including infrastructure investment, and aligning multi-annual strategic plans to annual budgets and medium-term priorities of governments
- adopting mechanisms that foster the efficient and transparent allocation of water-related public funds (e.g. through social contracts, scorecards and audits)
- minimising unnecessary administrative burdens related to public expenditure while preserving fiduciary and fiscal safeguards.

Evolving practices showcasing Principle 6:

- Payments for ecosystem services (PES) schemes, which are becoming a trend throughout Latin American countries, are a common instrument to raise the willingness-to-pay. Ring-fencing the use of revenues is key to stimulate self-financing in the water sector, since users experience the impacts of the measures implemented (Practices No. 22, 23 and 54).

- Water utilities in Kenya are highly inefficient (non-revenue water estimated at 43%) and in 2016 only 55% of the population had access to safe drinking water. The 2016 Water Act stipulates that all revenues generated in the water sector have to be invested in the water sector. One of Water Act objectives is to stimulate investments in the water services sector (Practice No. 27).
- In Tajikistan, setting-up public advisory councils in water supply companies has protected the rights and interests of consumers and encouraged their participation in the decision-making processes. During the public advisory council meetings, consumers present complaints and requests to water supply company management staff who provide explanations and commitment to resolve issues. Minutes and follow-up actions are later published on a website administered by the Consumers Union of Tajikistan. The costs of the services are communicated to the water service users and the level of the tariff is explained. This has resulted in an increase of mutual trust between the providers and the customers, and ultimately increased tariff collection (Practice No. 37).
- In Portugal, aligning multi-annual strategic plans to annual budgets and medium-term priorities of governments helped the continuity of water policies even cutting across political cycles. The six-year strategic plans guided the implementation of the country's water services public policy and were concomitant with EU funding under the umbrella of the Cohesion Funds and other EU programmes. The plan and its revisions every six years have followed a similar structure to ensure consistency, i.e. analysis of the current situation, identifying the gaps and defining the goals, quantifying the investment needs, identifying the measures needed, designing the implementation process of the strategies within the plan, and defining the monitoring instruments and intermediate reviews. The medium-term time frame implies that there is a need to reach consensus among political parties with different ideologies and also makes prominent the need to co-ordinate the plan with other environmental policies, for instance, water resources, energy, river basin planning, spatial planning, green growth, among others (Practice No. 51).
- In Zambia, placing water high on the development agenda by integrating water into national planning has unlocked investments in the water sector. Zambia has traditionally faced a number of challenges in managing water resources, including water supply shortages, pollution, inadequate information for decision making, inefficient use of water resources, and limited stakeholder awareness and participation. The 1994 water governance reform acknowledged that IWRM approaches were important to address these issues. In 2002, the Ministry of Energy and Water Development began developing an Integrated Water Resources Management and Water Efficiency (IWRM/WE) Plan to provide a "unified implementation plan that supports both the reforms of water resources management as well as all other inter-related/multi-sectoral aspects of IWRM and water efficiency, in a coordinated, effective and efficient manner." The integration of the IWRM/WE plan into the wider national development planning process has resulted in increased investment in water initiatives. There is a clear upward trend in the allocation of budget to the water sector – an increase of 44%, from ZMW 43 billion (Zambian kwacha) in 2013 to ZMW 62 billion in 2016. Additionally, the framework provided by the IWRM/WE plan has been used to embed overseas development funding into national planning frameworks. For example, in 2012 a grant of EUR 950 000 was awarded by the African Water

Facility of the African Development Bank to the Zambian government for a project on the development of multi-purpose small dams (identified as a priority area within the IWRM/WE plan). This was followed in 2013 by the World Bank financing of USD 50 million to the Zambian government for a Water Resources Development Project established as part of a programme of support to the implementation of the IWRM/WE plan (Practice No. 24).

Principle 7: Regulatory frameworks

Ensure that sound water management regulatory frameworks are effectively implemented and enforced in pursuit of the public interest, through:

- ensuring a comprehensive, coherent, and predictable legal and institutional framework that sets rules, standards and guidelines for achieving water policy outcomes, and encourages integrated long-term planning
- ensuring that key regulatory functions are discharged across public agencies, dedicated institutions and levels of government and that regulatory authorities are endowed with the necessary resources
- ensuring that rules, institutions and processes are well-co-ordinated, transparent, non-discriminatory, participative, and easy to understand and enforce
- encouraging the use of regulatory tools (evaluation and consultation mechanisms) to foster the quality of regulatory processes and make the results accessible to the public, where appropriate
- setting clear, transparent and proportionate enforcement rules, procedures, incentives and tools (including rewards and penalties) to promote compliance and achieve regulatory objectives in a cost-effective way
- ensuring that effective remedies can be claimed through non-discriminatory access to justice, considering the range of options as appropriate.

Evolving practices showcasing Principle 7:

- In Kenya, indicators are a common practice to promote compliance and achieve regulatory objectives in a cost-effective way. The Water Services Regulatory Board is responsible for setting and enforcing rules and standards for the water services sector ensuring that consumers are protected and have access to efficient, adequate, affordable and sustainable services. The Water Services Regulatory Board, with the support of GIZ, has developed a governance indicator that measures the level of compliance of Kenyan water utilities. The sub-indicators touch upon six dimensions: oversight and supervision, information and control systems, financial management, service standards, human resources, and customer consultation. The scores from the sub-indicators are aggregated and the final result of the governance indicator is reported in an annual performance report, which is made available to the public (Practice No. 27).
- In Panama, discriminatory and non-participative regulation had impacts on water policy outcomes, and non-discriminatory access to justice was key to changing those regulations. The Environmental Advocacy Centre of Panama, along with other environmental NGOs, filed a lawsuit against Panama's environmental flow regulation in early 2015. The NGO coalition argued that the regulation granted 90% of water flows to hydroelectric projects without considering the impacts this would have on ecosystems, and without consulting water users, particularly those

who depended directly on river flows to satisfy their domestic water needs. In December 2016, Panama's Supreme Court annulled the country's environmental flow regulation because it had been designed and approved without ensuring public participation (Practice No. 25).

Principle 8: Innovative governance

Promote the adoption and implementation of innovative water governance practices across responsible authorities, levels of government and relevant stakeholders, through:

- encouraging experimentation and pilot testing on water governance, drawing lessons from success and failures, and scaling-up replicable practices
- promoting social learning to facilitate dialogue and consensus-building, for example through networking platforms, social media, information and communication technologies, and user-friendly interfaces (e.g. digital maps, big data, smart data and open data) and other means
- promoting innovative ways to co-operate, pool resources and capacity, build synergies across sectors and search for efficiency gains, notably through metropolitan governance, inter-municipal collaboration, urban-rural partnerships and performance-based contracts
- promoting a strong science-policy interface to contribute to better water governance and bridge the divide between scientific findings and water governance practices.

Evolving practices showcasing Principle 8:

- In the Mediterranean region, GWP launched a Non-Conventional Water Resources (NCWR) Programme that, among others, promoted the upscale of local practices with the objective of incorporating them into local, subnational and national strategies. A tangible impact was seen in Malta, where the National Water Management Plan included NCWR solutions as part of the country's water security strategy (Practice No. 52).
- In Spain, the knowledge provided by the University of Murcia will help guide the measures taken to recover the fauna and flora of the Segura River. The Segura River Basin Authority is co-ordinating two LIFE+projects (co-funded by the EU) that involve local and regional administrations, an environmental NGO (ANSE), and the academic community (University of Murcia) (Practice No. 45).
- In Turkey, the water information system currently under development is expected to gather data, maps, statistics and policy documents, but most importantly to be based on a GIS tool to improve data visualisation and make the system more user-friendly to the broader public. The final National Water Information System will be integrated into Turkey's "E-government" system, an online public portal informing on the quality of public services. The ultimate objective is to promote social learning on water policy and encourage the use of data by non-governmental actors (i.e. academia, NGOs, etc.) (Practice No. 20).
- The Waves system is an open data initiative launched by Dutch Water Authorities to promote social learning in the Netherlands. Waves makes large amounts of data on the performance of each water authority available to the public. Every two years, Dutch Water Authorities analyses the data and publishes a report that benchmarks the performance of all the authorities. Besides the open data and the

reports, the website also provides tools that allow running simple analyses (Practice No. 17).

- In Colombia, behavioural change campaigns in the Valle de Cauca contributed to doubling the number of downstream water users implementing conservation measures. Fourteen staff of the local environmental authority trained community leaders on natural resource management, social marketing and campaign planning, while also building their capacity to create trust among different types of stakeholders. As a result, about 1 700 ha of forest are now protected voluntarily by landowners in the region. Valle de Cauca exceeded its annual conservation goal, deforestation rates sunk well below the national average and the watersheds see positive trends in the forest and water quality indices (Practice No. 54).

Principle 9: Integrity and transparency

Mainstream integrity and transparency practices across water policies, water institutions and water governance frameworks for greater accountability and trust in decision making, through:

- promoting legal and institutional frameworks that hold decision makers and stakeholders accountable, such as the right to information and independent authorities to investigate water-related issues and law enforcement
- encouraging norms, codes of conduct, or charters on integrity and transparency in national or local contexts and monitoring their implementation
- establishing clear accountability and control mechanisms for transparent water policy making and implementation
- diagnosing and mapping on a regular basis existing or potential drivers of corruption and risks in all water-related institutions at different levels, including for public procurement
- adopting multi-stakeholder approaches, dedicated tools and action plans to identify and address water integrity and transparency gaps (e.g. integrity scans/pacts, risk analysis, social witnesses).

Evolving practices showcasing Principle 9:

- Establishing clear accountability and control mechanisms is a key feature of the successful implementation of the Pipiripau PES scheme (Brazil). Several mechanisms have contributed to this. First, all formal and institutional documents are available for public consultation. Second, the *Official Diary of the Federal District* discloses all contracts for PES that are part of the scheme. Third, the expenditures carried out for improving the ecosystem services of the Pipiripau watershed are carried out through the SIGGO, which is the official payment system of the government of the federal district. Lastly, the multi-stakeholder approach followed by the project, which involves the federal and district administrations, NGOs, and water users, is perceived as a mutual control mechanism to ensure integrity (Practice No. 23).
- Tools such as the Climate Bonds Standard and Certification Scheme can help pool resources from financial markets. Climate bonds are part of a new and growing market that can boost water infrastructure investment to deal with climate change impacts. However, standards, assurance and certification will be essential to improve confidence and transparency, which in turn will enable

further strong growth in the market. The Climate Bonds Standard and Certification Scheme is a screening tool that allows investors and intermediaries to assess the climate integrity of certified climate bonds. The standard is a product of Climate Bonds Initiative and is developing water criteria that can help screen grey, hybrid and nature-based water infrastructure projects and assets (Practice No. 21).

- In Indonesia, the Jasa Tirta I Public Corporation (PJT1) has used norms and codes to mainstream integrity and transparency practices in its activities. Established in 1990, the PJT1 is a state-owned legally independent organisation that manages five river basins. The PJT1 has become a model of integrity for other Indonesian river basins. The PJT1 started mainstreaming integrity practices into its day-to-day activities back in 2002, when the corporation adopted the Indonesia Financial Accounting Standards and started submitting on a regular basis accountability reports to the Ministry of State Owned Enterprises. The PJT1 then implemented good corporate governance practices such as codes of conduct, integrity pacts and whistle-blowing mechanisms. Moreover, all employees must sign the corporation's integrity pact (Practice No. 30).
- The International Commission for the Protection of the Danube River has developed rules of procedure to mainstream integrity and transparency practices to increase accountability and trust in the decision-making process of the commission. These rules range from the fundaments of treaties to organisational rules for staff members of the permanent secretariat. The commission also supports the active involvement of stakeholders and civil society through observer organisations as well as public consultation processes for the development of basin management plans (Practice No. 31).

Principle 10: Stakeholder engagement

Promote stakeholder engagement for informed and outcome-oriented contributions to water policy design and implementation, through:

- mapping public, private and non-profit actors who have a stake in the outcome or who are likely to be affected by water-related decisions, as well as their responsibilities, core motivations and interactions
- paying special attention to under-represented categories (youth, the poor, women, indigenous people, domestic users) newcomers (property developers, institutional investors), and other water-related stakeholders and institutions
- defining the line of decision making and the expected use of stakeholders' inputs, and mitigating power imbalances and risks of consultation capture from over-represented or overly vocal categories, as well as between expert and non-expert voices
- encouraging capacity development of relevant stakeholders as well as accurate, timely and reliable information, as appropriate
- assessing the process and outcomes of stakeholder engagement to learn, adjust and improve accordingly, including the evaluation of costs and benefits of engagement processes
- promoting legal and institutional frameworks, organisational structures and responsible authorities that are conducive to stakeholder engagement, taking account of local circumstances, needs and capacities
- customising the type and level of stakeholder engagement to the needs and keeping the process flexible to adapt to changing circumstances.

Evolving practices showcasing Principle 10:

- In Karachi (Pakistan), stakeholder engagement has led to more effective implementation of water services policies and projects. The Karachi Water Partnership (KWP), formally launched in April 2007, brings government, private sector and civil society together. The core value of the KWP is that improving water services in the city is a shared responsibility across all stakeholder groups. During 2007-13, the KWP signed seven Memoranda of Understanding with local institutions for the implementation of water services projects (Practice No. 38).
- In Jordan, the government is integrating a bottom-up approach for water management to improve water policy outcomes. Based on a detailed stakeholder mapping, three working groups in refugee-hosting communities in the northern governorates (Samar, Foa'arah and Kharaj) have been established with the support of GIZ and meet regularly. The objective is to have a platform to express and voice stakeholders' interests and concerns, and to integrate the results of the dialogue into drinking water supply policies and water infrastructure planning processes (Practice No. 53).
- In Jordan, stakeholder engagement helped overcome tensions with local residents regarding the As Samra project. The As Samra project is the first build-operate-transfer contract in Jordan and first wastewater treatment facility in the Middle East to use a combination of private, local government and donor financing, including the United States Agency for International Development. The treatment plant serves 3.5 million people in Greater Amman and produces 100 million m^3 per year of high-quality water for irrigation in the Jordan Valley, which reduces the use of drinking water from fresh sources for crop irrigation. Additionally, the plant is almost self-sufficient in energy with an energy potential recovery of 80%; and the sludge recovered from the wastewater treatment can be recycled as fuel or as a fertiliser to rehabilitate soils. However, all these benefits did not necessarily enable a proper ownership and support of the project by all stakeholders, especially local residents. To solve this situation, the operator engaged proactively in a dialogue to clarify the causes of the issues and find solutions to solve them. The platform for this dialogue was an environmental committee that meets monthly and involves representatives of the Ministry of Water and Irrigation, the governor of Zarqa, the mayors of Balaama and Hashmiyya (main cities in the area), environmental industries, environmental associations, and farmers (Practice No. 48).
- Misalignment of interests across stakeholder groups in Rijnenburg (Netherlands) paralysed a promising residential project. In 2008, Rijnenburg, a new residential area near the city of Utrecht, joined forces with the provincial government and the Dutch Water Authority Stichtse Rijnlanden to come up with a sustainable urban design. The area was to become self-sufficient in terms of energy and water management, and the historical value of the landscape would be preserved. A wide range of stakeholders were involved in the design of the project, including a large number of public authorities, property developers, residents and NGOs. However, a reformulation of the plans reduced the number of houses to be constructed from 15 000 to 5 000-7 000. This lowered the profit expectations for property developers, and some claimed that they would even suffer losses. The project came to a stall in 2010 and has not been reactivated yet (Practice No. 36).

- In Kampen (Netherlands), engaging with civil society helped bridge capacity gaps of the public administration to deal with risks of too much water. A brigade consisting of 200 volunteers manages a flexible flood protection system when the water rises. The Water Authority of Drents Overijsselse Delta is in charge of co-ordinating these actions. The system stretches over 2 kilometres of historical urban area and has 84 spots with stop-logs and valves (Practice No. 34).

Principle 11: Trade-offs across users, rural and urban areas, and generations

Encourage water governance frameworks that help manage trade-offs across water users, rural and urban areas, and generations, through:

- promoting non-discriminatory participation in decision making across people, especially vulnerable groups and people living in remote areas
- empowering local authorities and users to identify and address barriers to access quality water services and resources and promoting rural-urban co-operation, including through greater partnership between water institutions and spatial planners
- promoting public debate on the risks and costs associated with too much, too little or too polluted water to raise awareness, build consensus on who pays for what, and contribute to better affordability and sustainability now and in the future
- encouraging evidence-based assessment of the distributional consequences of water-related policies on citizens, water users and places to guide decision making.

Evolving practices showcasing Principle 11:

- In Lima (Peru) and Castellon (Spain), an academic institution produced evidence and raised awareness among local stakeholders on the distributional consequences of water and sanitation services policies on vulnerable groups (children, teenagers, women groups). The goal of the projects was to raise awareness on certain data dimensions of access to and quality of water services that are often overlooked in aggregated data at metropolitan scale (i.e. data by neighbourhood). The assessment was based on the five components of the Human Right to Water and Sanitation (availability, accessibility, quality and safety, affordability, and acceptability). The results have not yet triggered any public policy initiatives, but they have raised awareness among local stakeholders on the risk of exclusion of vulnerable groups in water services policies at metropolitan level (Practices No. 39 and 40).
- In the Fitzroy River basin (Australia), the OECD Principles are providing a tool for under-represented stakeholders groups to promote their engagement in water policy design and implementation. An indigenous community from Australia has developed a political declaration aiming to protect the traditional and environmental values that underpin the Fitzroy River's heritage. The aboriginal community has been the traditional guardian of the river for centuries, but increasing development in the watershed is jeopardising the future of the river and its people. The "Fitzroy River Declaration", which has been developed based on the OECD Principles, urges the government to set up a governance system in Western Australia that allows for greater stakeholder engagement and ultimately joint management of the river between the government and aboriginal communities (Practice No. 41).

- In Chad, empowering water users' associations in rural areas helped identify and address barriers to access quality water services. The government created a Support and Advisory Unit for Management (CCAG) to support the water users' associations, given their low level of capacities and resources. The CCAG is financed by the water users' associations and its mission is to provide technical services and financial monitoring to improve the quality and sustainability of water services. To this end, the CCAG conducts field missions to gather data and produce technical and financial indicators that feature into reports submitted to the ministry and the water users' associations. NGOs in the field also play a key role by providing technical, financial and organisational trainings to the CCAG. One of the priorities of these trainings is to provide the right skills to manage trade-offs across local stakeholders (Practice No. 42).

Principle 12: Monitoring and evaluation

Promote regular monitoring and evaluation of water policy and governance where appropriate, share the results with the public and make adjustments when needed, through:

- promoting dedicated institutions for monitoring and evaluation that are endowed with sufficient capacity, the appropriate degree of independence and resources as well as the necessary instruments
- developing reliable monitoring and reporting mechanisms to effectively guide decision making
- assessing to what extent water policy fulfils the intended outcomes and that water governance frameworks are fit for purpose
- encouraging timely and transparent sharing of the evaluation results and adapting strategies as new information becomes available.

Evolving practices showcasing Principle 12:

- In Portugal, to support the implementation of water services policies, the Water and Waste Services Regulation Authority (ERSAR) implemented a system of performance indicators (16 for drinking water supply services and 16 for urban wastewater management services) to assess the quality of service provided. The system started back in 2004 only for concessional services, and since 2011 all water service operators are registered. The results of the indicators for each service provider are assessed and benchmarked against other service providers. The information is made publicly available and feeds official national and European statistics, as well as relevant policy discussions and decisions. It guides the elaboration and review of the national strategic plans for water services (Practice No. 51).
- Ireland conducted a comprehensive review (in 2010 and 2014) to assess to what extent water policy fulfils the intended outcomes. Out of this came the creation of a new three-tier interlocking governance structure described in earlier sections with a much stronger focus on collaboration, role clarity, hard science and evidence, integrated catchment management, and public engagement. Ireland is committed to continue evaluating these structures as they evolve and making changes where they make sense from a policy and operational viewpoint (Practice No. 49).

- In the United Republic of Tanzania, a self-assessment tool helps evaluate whether catchment-based institutions are delivering their mandate. Tanzania has nine basin water boards that implement IWRM at basin level. The basin water boards are decentralised administrative units, which together with catchment committees and water users' associations make up the institutional framework for water resources management. The Performance Assessment Framework (PAF) is a self-assessment tool that supports basin water boards to regularly assess their performance against their institutional mandate. The tool was developed by the Ministry of Water and Irrigation with the support of GIZ. The Ministry provides support to the boards when conducting the PAF, which is also an excellent opportunity for the ministry to map the strengths and weaknesses of each board. The PAF helps water boards identify their gaps and strategically plan measures to overcome them. The PAF is also used to report back to the Water Sector Development Programme, a joint initiative between international partners and the government to improve the water sector overall (Practice No. 43).

Peer learning through thematic webinars

The set of evolving practices is a way forward to support the implementation of the OECD Principles by scaling-up practices that can help governments and stakeholders move from vision to action. The evolving practices show experiences of countries at various levels (local, basin, national) that could help identify ways forward for the implementation of the OECD Principles. In particular, these experiences capture the "what" (policy and legal frameworks), the "who" (institutions) and the "how" (instruments).

Evolving practices provide a vehicle for peer-to-peer dialogue and learning, and thematic webinars are a useful tool to support this process. A discussion on evolving practices provides the opportunity to gather a small group of practitioners around the table to share their experiences and discuss ways forward to overcome water challenges. Webinars are a useful tool to support this experience-sharing exercise where practice providers come from different countries and/or continents. The OECD WGI conducted four of these webinars (findings are presented in Box 3.1).

Drawing on the results of the four webinars, the OECD has developed a set of "steps" that aim to provide guidance on how to carry out peer-learning webinars. These "steps" recommend that a lead institution take responsibility for defining the topic and choosing the practices discussion during the webinar. They also identify the necessary framework conditions to make the discussion useful for policy makers and stakeholders. The aim is to trigger true dialogue amongst different parties around evolving practices under the umbrella of a given topic.

- **Step 1: Identify a lead institution.** It is best for webinars to be hosted by a lead institution to ensure ownership of the exercise. The lead institution should be responsible for defining the topic of the webinar and choosing the practices to be discussed.
- **Step 2: Set clear rules.** To facilitate dialogue and exchange of experiences limit the number of participants per webinar (10-15 people) and keep discussions to 90-120 minutes. Moreover, it is key to encourage participants to listen actively, avoid judgemental statements, show openness to share and consider a "Chatham House" rule during the exchanges.

Box 3.1. Peer-to-peer dialogue and exchange on the practices

The main outcomes of the peer-learning webinars can be dived into four themes:

1. **Prominent governance enablers on the ground:** 1) effective stakeholder engagement creates ownership among stakeholders (private sector, citizens, local administrations, service providers, etc.), can bridge capacity gaps, reduces conflicts among different categories of stakeholders, and can drive innovations; 2) mobilising the necessary financial resources is a key feature to effective policy implementation; 3) strong political support is the key driver for success of water governance reforms and projects. Other lessons drawn from the webinars is that water governance in highly contextualised and that better data and information help adjust water governance frameworks to achieve policy objectives.
2. **Improving water governance at large.** The importance of moving from using the OECD Principles as a retrospective assessment framework towards an approach where the Principles are used to help determine whether water governance systems are fit to face future challenges and changing conditions (population growth, increased flood risk, water scarcity, climate change, etc.) was underscored. To monitor governance processes under changing frameworks, alternative data – such as the commitment or satisfaction of stakeholders – should complement more traditional data sources (hydrological or water quality data). The latter could be possibly done through the OECD Water Governance Indicators (see Chapter 2). Lastly, the global agenda and commitments provide a window of opportunity to place governance as the means for implementation.
3. **Transferability of practices.** It could be concluded that the webinars were a useful first step to find out which elements from different practices can shed light on the challenges faced by a specific participant. Among these elements, participants highlighted that pitfalls to avoid were the most useful during the discussions. Practices are more likely to be useful when they deal with similar challenges or problems to the ones that should be addressed or solved. The importance of the context and the transferability of the evolving practices should be discussed and analysed through further bilateral conversations and thorough analysis. Thus, it was pointed out that practices that are successful in one context should not just be copied into another context, but rather the different contexts should be analysed and the solution tailored as appropriate.
4. **How to learn through webinars.** Basic guidelines and rules can help foster peer-to-peer learning through the webinars. First, the presentations of the practices and the discussions should be strongly focused on how the evolving practice can be useful for others or how it could be used in the future. Second, a peer-reviewed structure of the presentation by the webinar organiser helps drive consistency when presenting the critical elements of the different practices (i.e. the structure used for these webinars was: overview, OECD Principles showcased, main challenges and ways forward). Third, practices must be shared in advance with all participants so that they are familiar with the practice prior to the webinar. Thus, time for the presentation should be limited and focus on the key messages to allow for in-depth discussions. Lastly, each participant should present a simplified SWOT analysis of the practice of another participant. The latter allows focusing the discussions on what is of interest for each participant.

Box 3.1. **Peer-to-peer dialogue and exchange on the practices** (*continued*)

Table 3.3. **The scope of the four peer-learning webinars**

Webinar	Host institution	Evolving practices discussed
The new role of cities in urban water governance	Flanders Knowledge Center Water	"Participatory diagnosis of access to water and sanitation services of vulnerable stakeholder groups: The case of Lima (Peru)" "Promoting behavioural change in urban water consumption in Flanders (Belgium)" "Climate bonds: An innovative financial tool for the water sector" "Sustainable solutions for climate-resilient cities through public-private partnerships (Alicante, Spain)" "A governance framework to implement alternative water supply solutions in the Mediterranean region"
Stakeholder engagement for effective water governance	SUEZ	"Using the OECD Principles to engage under-represented stakeholder groups in water governance: Fitzroy River Declaration" "Increasing climate resiliency through stakeholder engagement in the Netherlands" "Overcoming conflict in a wastewater project in Jordan through stakeholder engagement"
Governance of wastewater and water reuse, and the role for innovation	Israel Water Authority	"Israel sewage information systems: An innovative water quality policy instrument" and "Implementing wastewater reuse policies in Israel" "SANePLAN (Life Program of European Commission): Ensuring policy coherence across sanitation services and urban planning (Spain and Italy)" "Framework conditions to favour the water-energy nexus in Vienna" "Implementation of a public policy for water services: The case of Portugal"
Water governance in river basins	Association of public services and enterprises and Federal Ministry of Agriculture, Forestry, Environment and Water Management (Austria)	"Co-ordinating an environmental recovery plan in the Segura River (Spain)" "Evolving water governance to ensure drinking water supply in Vienna (Austria)" "Water Fund: A governance and financing mechanism for the Camboriu watershed (Brazil)" "Implementation of integrated water resources management approach in the Chikugo River Basin (Japan)" "Alternative approach to river basin governance in Austria"

- **Step 3: Set a clear structure.** The event should start with a scene-setting overview by the host, including the webinar topic, rationale and expected outcomes. It should also include an explanation of why the host is organising the webinar. Second, each practice provider presents a brief overview of their practice. The presentations are then followed by a group discussion during which all webinar participants and practice providers are invited to intervene.
- **Step 4: Ensure focused presentations and a structured discussion.** The presentations of the practices should focus on the related OECD Principles, main governance challenges and ways forward to overcome those challenges (lessons learnt and pitfalls to avoid). The presentations and the discussions should also be strongly focused on how the evolving practice can be useful for others and/or how it could be used in the future. A peer-reviewed structure of the presentation by the webinar host can help drive consistency when presenting the critical elements of the different practices.

- **Step 5: Share all relevant material in advance.** Share rules, structure of the discussion and evolving practices sufficiently in advance with all participants so that they are familiar with them prior to the webinar.
- **Step 6: Follow-up after the exchange and draw lessons to improve practices and policies.** Following the webinars, the host institution(s) should fill out a post-event report designed to reveal the potential for peer learning through structured dialogue around evolving water governance practices. The report seeks to gain insights on the type of cross-cutting lessons that can be extracted from the dialogue and provides an opportunity to identify follow-up actions.

Note

1. Note by Turkey: The information in this document with reference to "Cyprus" relates to the southern part of the Island. There is no single authority representing both Turkish and Greek Cypriot people on the Island. Turkey recognises the Turkish Republic of Northern Cyprus (TRNC). Until a lasting and equitable solution is found within the context of the United Nations, Turkey shall preserve its position concerning the "Cyprus issue". Note by all the European Union Member States of the OECD and the European Union: The Republic of Cyprus is recognised by all members of the United Nations with the exception of Turkey. The information in this document relates to the area under the effective control of the Government of the Republic of Cyprus.

References

OECD (2016a), "OECD inventory of best practices databases", unpublished.

OECD (2016b), "What do you look for when searching for best practices and case studies on water governance?", survey, OECD, Paris, www.oecd.org/cfe/regional-policy/OECD-WGI-survey-best-practices.pdf.

Annex 3.A1.
List of respondents to the survey on practices

Table 3.A1.1. **List of respondents to the survey on practices**

Organisation/institution	Area/detail
Africa Water Watch Ltd	Africa
Asian Development Bank	Asia
Network of Asian River Basin Organizations (NARBO)	Asia
GWMWater	Australia
Austrian Development Agency	Austria
Fresh Thoughts Consulting GmbH	Austria
Federal Ministry of Agriculture, Forestry, Environment and Water Management	Austria
Social Watch Benin	Benin
University of Sarajevo – Faculty of Mechanical Engineering	Bosnia and Herzegovina
Comitê das Bacias Hidrográficas do Litoral Norte	Brazil
IPH/UFGRS	Brazil
Ministry of the Environment	Brazil
University of Sao Paulo – School of Engineering of Sao Carlos	Brazil
Federal University of São Carlos (UFSCar)	Brazil
Observatory of Water Governance	Brazil
Associacao de Moradores do Alto da Gavea	Brazil
Ministry of Industry, Foreign Trade and Services	Brazil
Agency Peixe Vivo	Brazil
Comitê das Bacias Hidrográficas do Rio Jamari	Brazil
River Basin Committee of Paraiba do Sul	Brazil
Institute for Applied Economic Research (IPEA)	Brazil
Government of Northwest Territories	Canada
Ministère du Développement durable, de l'Environnement et de la Lutte contre les changements climatiques de Quebec	Canada
International Secretariat for Water	Canada
Ministry of Public Works	Chile
Superintendency of Sanitary Services	Chile
Green Zhejiang	China (People's Republic of)
Confederation of Danish Industry	Denmark
Programme Solidarité Eau (pS-Eau)	France
Initiative Developpement	France
Agence Française de Développement (AFD)	France
Plan bleu	France
Université Paris VIII – UNIGE	France
University of Paris (Pantheon-Sorbonne)	France
ENGIE	France
Morija Organisation	France
Collectif Eau	France
France Hydro Electricity	France
CILE (Compagnie Intercommunale Liégeoise des Eaux)	France
SDEA Alsace Moselle	France
Secours Islamique France	France
GIZ	Germany
Dreisam SpA	Germany

Table 3.A1.1. **List of respondents to the survey on practices** (*continued*)

Organisation/institution	Area/detail
Muslim Family Counselling Services	Ghana
Minister of Foreign Affairs	Guatemala
Downstream Dialogue	Independent expert
Guillermo Madariaga	Independent expert
Banka BioLoo	India
AquaFed	International
International Labour Organization	International
Organisation for Economic Co-operation and Development	International
International Water Association (IWA)	International
Food and Agriculture Organization of the United Nations	International
Global Water Operators' Partnerships Alliance/UN-Habitat	International
UNESCO-IHE (Institute for Water Education)	International
International Network of Basin Organisations	International
International Joint Commission (Canada-US)	International
World Bank	International
International Association for Water Law	International
UN-REDD Programme	International
Veolia	International
Water Integrity Network	International
WWF International	International
Shahid Beheshti University	Iran
Association of Environmental Justice in Israel	Israel
Consulting Engs.	Israel
Ministry of Economy	Israel
Water Authority Tuscany	Italy
City of Bologna	Italy
City of Milano	Italy
Ministry of Water and Irrigation	Jordan
Permanent Delegation of the Republic of Korea to the OECD	Korea
Ministry of Environment	Korea
University of Malta	Malta
National Commission of Water (CONAGUA)	Mexico
Dutch Water Authority De Dommel	Netherlands
Leiden University College	Netherlands
NETWERC H2O	Netherlands
Municipality of Roermond	Netherlands
Association of Insurers	Netherlands
University of Utrecht – KWR Watercycle Research Institute	Netherlands
Women for Water Partnership	Netherlands
Waternet	Netherlands
Deltares	Netherlands
Waterschap vallei en veluwe	Netherlands
Landcare Research	New Zealand
Universidad Nacional de Jaén	Peru
National Water Authority	Peru
Upholding Life And Nature (ULAN)	Philippines
INDAQUA – Indústria e Gestão de Água, S.A.	Portugal
TPF Planege Cenor	Portugal
Water and waste services regulation authority	Portugal
Aguas Ribatejo	Portugal
SMAS DE TOMAR	Portugal

Table 3.A1.1. **List of respondents to the survey on practices** (*continued*)

Organisation/institution	Area/detail
Portuguese Water Partnership (PWP)	Portugal
Sisaqua	Portugal
Green Echoes Association	Romania
Taibah University and Environmental Agency	Saudi Arabia
Water Witness International	Scotland, United Kingdom
National Water Agency	Slovenia
Department of Water and Santation	South Africa
AWARD	South Africa
University of Valencia – Faculty of Physics	Spain
AQUAE Foundation	Spain
Aguas de Valencia, S.A	Spain
Metropolitan Area of Barcelona	Spain
Sercomosa	Spain
Spanish Association of Water Supply and Sanitation	Spain
Adecagua	Spain
Technical University of Catalonia	Spain
Jucar River Basin Authority	Spain
Institute of Technology, University of Moratuwa	Sri Lanka
Swedish International Development Co-operation Agency	Sweden
University of Geneva	Switzerland
WaterLex	Switzerland
Ernst Basler + Partner AG	Switzerland
ACoNPE/H-Lif	Tunisia
Hydropolitics Academy Association	Turkey
Uganda Coalition for Sustainable Development	Uganda
Ministry of Water and Environment (Water and Sanitation Development Facility - North)	Uganda
Arup	United Kingdom
Water Policy International	United Kingdom
Scottish government	United Kingdom
South Nation River Conservation Authority (Eastern Ontario)	United States
The Coca-Cola Company	United States
Texas A&M University	United States
University of Texas at Austin	United States
Kent County	United States
United States Agency for International Development	United States
University of Arizona – Water Resources Research Center	United States
University of Pennsylvania	United States
Office of Native American and International Affairs in the Bureau of Reclamation	United States
US Geological Survey	United States

ORGANISATION FOR ECONOMIC CO-OPERATION AND DEVELOPMENT

The OECD is a unique forum where governments work together to address the economic, social and environmental challenges of globalisation. The OECD is also at the forefront of efforts to understand and to help governments respond to new developments and concerns, such as corporate governance, the information economy and the challenges of an ageing population. The Organisation provides a setting where governments can compare policy experiences, seek answers to common problems, identify good practice and work to co-ordinate domestic and international policies.

The OECD member countries are: Australia, Austria, Belgium, Canada, Chile, the Czech Republic, Denmark, Estonia, Finland, France, Germany, Greece, Hungary, Iceland, Ireland, Israel, Italy, Japan, Korea, Latvia, Luxembourg, Mexico, the Netherlands, New Zealand, Norway, Poland, Portugal, the Slovak Republic, Slovenia, Spain, Sweden, Switzerland, Turkey, the United Kingdom and the United States. The European Union takes part in the work of the OECD.

OECD Publishing disseminates widely the results of the Organisation's statistics gathering and research on economic, social and environmental issues, as well as the conventions, guidelines and standards agreed by its members.

OECD PUBLISHING, 2, rue André-Pascal, 75775 PARIS CEDEX 16
(42 2018 24 1 P) ISBN 978-92-64-29266-6 – 2018

www.ingramcontent.com/pod-product-compliance
Lightning Source LLC
Chambersburg PA
CBHW080757150926
51501CB00045B/1262
* 9 7 8 9 2 6 4 2 9 2 6 6 6 *